Princeton Theological Monograph Series

Dikran Y. Hadidian

General Editor

35

THE LITTLE CHURCH THAT
REFUSED TO DIE

WILLIAM W. MOORE

THE LITTLE CHURCH THAT REFUSED TO DIE

PICKWICK PUBLICATIONS
ALLISON PARK, PENNSYLVANIA

Published by
Pickwick Publications
4137 Timberlane Drive
Allison Park, PA 15101-2932
USA

Printed on Acid Free Paper in the United States of America

Library of Congress Cataloging-in-Publication Data

Moore, William W.
    The little church that refused to die / William W. Moore.
       p. 134   cm. -- (Princeton theological monograph series ; 35)
    Includes bibliographical references.
    ISBN 1-55635-023-6
    1. Arminian Nunnery--History. 2. Societies living in common without vows--England--Cambridgeshire--History. 3. Cambridge-shire (England)--Church history. I. Title. II. Series
BR753.A75M66   1993
274.26'54--dc20   93-30950
                                             CIP

ACKNOWLEDGMENTS

I am indebted to some special people who contributed to this work: the Reference Librarian at the Perkins School of Theology, Southern Methodist University, Laura H. Randall, for her careful guidance through a massive collection of church and theological literature; to the several residents at the Community of Little Gidding for their help, especially Pat Saunders and Sarah Van de Weyer, who allowed me access to several source documents about the early history of that sacred place. In particular, I want to express appreciation to two other women who contributed their talents: Lucy Morgan, a lovely artist and friend who did the cover design; Ruth Tabor Moore: wife, friend, coworker, reader, editor par excellence. Without her love and help I would be lost.

CONTENTS

INTRODUCTION

In the mid-seventeenth century the English Parliament received a resolution excoriating a place called THE ARMINIAN NUNNERY. Several years later during the English Civil War, the Army of Parliament ransacked and torched the place. In the mid-twentieth century, the distinquished poet, T. S. Eliot won the Nobel Prize for Literature for a series of poems he had written, one of which was about a place called LITTLE GIDDING, a remarkable but strange religious community built around a small church. In the mid-1980s, quite by accident, I discovered that THE ARMINIAN NUNNERY and LITTLE GIDDING were the same place!

Recent histories of the community, of which there are several, deny the existence of an 'Arminian Nunnery'— a phrase we shall soon discover that was intended to be abusive, not pious. Further, they maintain that Little Gidding was a Christian commune that existed for only a period of between twelve to thirty-two years, depending upon which history you favor. From my examination of the records of Little Gidding over the past several years, I concluded that it has been in existence in one form or another for almost a thousand years—and that some wonderful and unusual people have been involved in its story. They are so unusual that I decided to let their spirits speak for themselves.

In a time when churches all over are rife with strife over questions of doctrine, ordination, and other matters of what I call "churchianity," perhaps this story will provide some perspective on the durability of Christianity.

* * * * *

As will become apparent, it is appropriate to begin the story with some comments about T. S. Eliot and his work. On September 7, 1941, just three months to the day before the Japanese attacked Pearl Harbor, an American, who had by choice become a British subject and who was known at the time as the "literary dictator" of London, left that tormented city and moved to the suburbs. His objective was to escape the bombing blitz which had begun that month in even more deadly earnest after several years of incessant bombing by that more virulent dictator, Adolf Hitler.

The American turned Britisher, born Thomas Stearns Eliot in St. Louis, Missouri, one of the most famous men of letters of all time, came from a well-to-do family whose ancestors had left England during the puritan revolution of the seventeenth century. They had settled in New England but later moved to the midwest. As a teen-ager, Eliot had visited England and immediately fell in love with the country of his ancestors. Determined to come back some day, he did so as soon as he completed his studies at Harvard University. It was not until he was thirty-nine years old and well accepted in British society that he chose to give up his American citizenship and become an Englishman.

A tall, handsome, highly intelligent, nervous and exhausted man in his late forties, Eliot had tried being an air-raid warden but the constant loss of sleep caused by the incessant bombing of London, plus his fantasies that a bomb would land one night on top of his house and destroy him and his beloved books and manuscripts drove him to flee the city for the suburbs.

A poet and playwright of world renown, Eliot had a second objective in mind: to seek refuge in a friend's house in Guildford; a safe distance from London —if such were possible in those nightmarish times. For several years he had been attempting to complete an experiment he had started earlier: to convey through poetry not so much religious beliefs but what believing in religion did to one. To do so, Eliot found he had to deal with the world of the living as well as the world of the spirits; of life and death; and the inner turmoil of half guessing and half understanding but still, at the same time, having faith in one's beliefs. This is not an uncommon dilemma for anyone who tries to be true to one's self and to one's Creator.

To understand what Eliot was attempting to achieve, it is necessary to know something of his early religious background. While most of his English ancestors were puritan, those who emigrated to the United States and settled in the midwestern United States were Unitarians who rejected the traditional Christian belief in the Holy Trinity and the Divinity of Christ. It should be noted that John Calvin, from whom English Protestantism descended, abhorred the concepts of the Unitarians and would have nothing to do with them or their beliefs. Thus, the dichotomy between the beliefs of his ancestors and his early religious training may explain why Eliot's earliest writings were filled with a strange kind of symbolism that appeared to reflect an intense personal struggle with the beliefs of the church in which he was raised and his search for a different religious experience.

When he had reached his early forties—the age when one begins to wonder what life is really all about and the time when depression can easily occur—he made a major decison. He rejected Unitarianism and joined the Church of England. Almost immediately, his poetry began to reflect this conversion. His first poem after this religious event was entitled *Ash Wednesday* and was completely different from his earlier works. In it he introduced what he characterized as an "enlightener" whose purpose was to help mediate between the conscious world and the inner world of the spirit. From that poem on, his poetic works and dramas became a valiant effort to deal with the inseparability of life and death.

And so it was in that terrible month of September, 1941, T. S. Eliot left London not only for his own safety and that of his literary works, but also with a burning desire to complete a project he had been working on for over five years. No one who has not lived through a world at war can ever realize how a person's outlook is foreshortened; or how one tends to think that life exists only from day to day (especially when three thousand of one's neighbors have been killed in one month, as happened to Eliot). So this brilliant, troubled man began writing against time and with great anxiety for his and the world's future.

As the setting for the fourth and final poem in his project, he chose a small village with a tiny church in rural England which he had visited five years before when he had first conceived the idea of writing a series of poems about English villages. The village was located among three villages known as the Giddings: Great Gidding, Steeple Gidding, and Little Gidding. Located in the beautiful countryside of north Cambridgeshire some seventy miles northeast of London, Little Gidding is the last place one would think of as inspiring a great work of art, let alone a resolution by Parliament condemning it.

It consists of a group of small houses surrounding a large, rather nondescript manor house with the tiny church off by itself next to a pond on the edge of a nearby field and easily overlooked. The edifice is so small it more accurately should be called a chapel. But its size is not its strangest part. The interior is such that a book on church architecture in the British Library has difficulty describing it: ". . . the interior of the church at Little Gidding is strange and confusing. . . even the furnishings seem to defy source or country of origin. . . as does the foundation of the building itself which is lost in antiquity."

Although there is no suggestion in his poem that he knew of The Arminian Nunnery, Eliot may have been drawn to use Little Gidding as the setting for his poem because of the feeling one has that it is a place where time and timelessness exist side by side. Just sitting in the little church, for instance, gives one the sensation of being transported back in time. The experience makes it easier to understand why the central portion of his poem is a conversation with a ghost!

> '. . . a familiar and compound ghost, both inti-
> mate and unidentifiable. . . .' A ghost he chal-
> lenges: '. . . Speak, I may not comprehend, may
> not remember . . . ' But alas, the ghost turns him
> aside:
> 'I am not eager to rehearse my thought and theo-
> ry which you have forgotten. These things have
> served their purpose: let them be. . . and pray
> they be forgiven by others, as I pray you to for-
> give both bad and good . . .'

Such a conversation with a disembodied spirit in a quiet chapel in the midlands of England may seem strange to most Americans, but that is not the case with the people of the British Isles—the audience to whom Eliot, at the time, was directing his poem.

Although scarcely known to Americans, ghosts are not unknown to the people of Great Britain. For over 2,000 years the British Isles have been known to historians as the islands of ghosts. Early Mediterranean civilizations believed that these islands in the west were the place where the souls of the dead resided—a sort of Heaven where one enjoyed an idyllic life after death.

Of interest, too, is the fact that Eliot's most famous drama, *MURDER IN THE CATHEDRAL*, written before he completed the poem about Little Gidding, is a dramatization of the murder of Thomas a' Becket, the Archbishop of Canterbury. It is the ghost of Thomas a' Becket which is the first ever recorded in English history, having been first seen by a priest in 1241 objecting to repairs being made to the Cathedral.

So it could well be that when Eliot was faced with a phenomenon of a small but mysterious place he used the medium of a ghost to try and explain the unexplainable. Little Gidding certainly falls into that category. To this day, even though it has been the subject of numerous publications, it still remains unknown even to residents of the near-by communities—and to most of the world. The mystery was not even allayed when his masterwork containing the poem about the community, entitled FOUR QUARTETS, won the Nobel Prize for Literature in 1948 and he became the Poet Laureate of England.

The poem about Little Gidding is as difficult to comprehend as the community itself. Indeed, it is obtuse even to those who have tried to plumb its deeper meaning. But once I visited the community and the tiny church I began to understand what Eliot was attempting to convey. And I, too, was consumed by a need to know more about this place. What I discovered astounded me.

At the outset, I wish to make clear that this story is dedicated to the memory of T. S. Eliot because until I deciphered his poem, I failed to understand the deeper significance of this strange community. I am indebted to him, too, for the methodology of this work. Narrative is seldom the form of an historical work. But Eliot, early in his writing of *LITTLE GIDDING*, found it was a ghost who accosted him, and engaged him in a dialogue. The ghosts I met startled me at first, as I know they may startle you. But as I was drawn into a dialogue with them I relaxed and listened, sensing they meant me no harm. In fact they had much to tell and I missed them when they left me.

I confess to being disturbed by the emphasis on the negative which emerges in recounting the story of Little Gidding. I would have wished it otherwise. But then I consoled myself that much of history is like reading the daily newspaper, leaning heavily on calamity and crisis, violence and death. I trust that in the end you will be as moved as I have been to find how much this tiny place has been through in almost a thousand years and yet is still considered hallowed ground: quietly serene, aware that the legend over the doorway of the church as you enter says all that needs to be said:

THIS IS NONE OTHER BUT THE HOUSE
OF GOD AND THE GATE OF HEAVEN

I

THE SWORD AND THE MITER

It was on a rather dismal, cloudy day that I visited the small sanctuary to begin to fathom its mysteries and to try to understand why T. S. Eliot had found it so compelling. As I stood in the doorway, I noticed a small brass plaque on the wall over one of the benches. It seemed to have been mounted on the wall only recently. Its shiny newness was quite evident. The engraving on it was so small one almost needed a magnifying glass to read it.

The plaque contained a listing of the names of the patrons of the church and the dates of their patronage. The entries surprised me as I am sure they would have Eliot. The dates began early in the thirteenth century. Before examining the plaque more closely, I studied the interior of the church. It was small: fourteen feet wide, seventeen feet high and some fifty feet from door to altar. From front door to chancel, the north and south walls were lined with a single row of narrow benches facing the aisle, much like choir stalls in cathedrals. The furnishings while traditional seemed strange. Near the chancel was a large lectern topped by a brass eagle with wings outstretched but the talons on its claws were broken off. A Processional pole topped by a small crucifix with a medieval figure above it was leaning against the wall near the altar. Near the front door stood a large baptismal font, the cover of which had etched on it two *fleur de lis* and two eight-pointed crosses.

The only available light came through four windows; two on each side of the nave. Even with the poor

7

light of this overcast day, I noticed an inscription over the chancel, on either side of which were crosses which had eight-points but were more splayed in design than the sharp-pointed crosses on the baptismal font. The inscription read:

O FOR THE PEACE OF JERUSALEM

The legend and the crosses over the chancel jogged my memory. I walked to the brass plaque and studied it more closely. The first date on the plaque was 1225 and the first patron was the Grand Master of Knights Templar in England, Robert Songford. The next two names were those of the Grand Masters who succeeded him: Roscelyn de Ros and Robert de Turville. This had been a Templar church; a rare thing to find anywhere in England, let alone in a small hamlet in the midlands. As a Templar church, it should have been rounded with a turret-like structure on top!

I was surprised at the discovery. The brass plaque was so recently installed I doubted Eliot had known of this early history. But he must have guessed at it since he wrote:

> ... See, now they vanish, the faces and places,
> with the self which, as it could, loved them to
> become renewed, transfigured, in another pat-
> tern ...

It is doubtful, too, that he was aware that its first patrons were known as knight mystics who, clad in a white mantle with an eight-pointed cross over the heart, fought and died by the thousands for Christianity, and about whom there are as many myths as facts. These same Knights in Sir Walter Scott's, *IVANHOE,* are depicted as haughty and arrogant bullies; greedy and hypocritical despots who manipulated the affairs of countries and kings. But, strangely, in the epic poem, *PARZIVAL,* they are given the exalted status as guardians of the Holy Grail.

As I pondered this contradiction, I heard a sound at

the front of the church. I turned and looked into the gloomy recesses of the chancel. Was it the influence of Eliot's conversation with a ghost or was someone sitting on the bench under the legend above the altar? The eerie silence was broken by a quiet, thin voice:

"I am Hugh de Payen, founder of the Order of the Poor Knights of Christ and the Temple of Solomon."

I held my breath not knowing whether to speak or run out the door. It could not be happening that I was about to repeat Eliot's experience of holding a conversation with a ghost! Or could it?

The voice spoke again not seeming to be aware of my fright.

"There are many stories about our Order, most of them untrue. We did not repudiate Christ nor trample and spit on His cross. Our only reason for existence was to keep the roads and highways in the Holy Land safe for the protection of the pilgrims who visited the Holy City . . ."

I started to say something but realized my visitor continued to talk.

"Do not interrupt," the spirit said with some asperity.

I remained silent.

"Before I tell you some of the history of Knights Templar and the part they Played in the history of England and many other countries, I should correct the listings on that brass plaque. This church was given to the Knights Templar, seventy years before the date on that plaque. Maude Engayne, the widow of John Engayne, himself a Knight of the Order, transferred the property, including the

church, to the Temple Bruer—a Preceptory of the Knights Templar for this region in 1185. The first patron was Geoffrey Fitz-Stephen, who was the Grand Master of the Templars in England at the time."

"The history of the Templars began some sixty years before the date on that plaque in 1118 when I, along with eight other men, mostly middle aged, presented ourselves at the Palace of Baudouin I, King of Jerusalem, whose elder brother, Godfroi, had captured the city at the turn of the twelfth century, nineteen years before our arrival. His Majesty received us most cordially and sent for the Patriarch of Jerusalem, Heraclius, who served as the special emissary of the Pope to the Holy City. To our surprise and pleasure we immediately had placed at our disposal a small wing of the palace. We knew that God was with us when we discovered the wing to have been built over the foundation of the ancient temple of Solomon."

The last phrase seemed to be expressed in an attitude of prayer and the voice of the almost invisible speaker dropped to a whisper and stopped. In the silence that followed, my mind became filled with myriad thoughts. The last words of the shadowy figure in the front of the church, not more than thirty feet from where I sat, had triggered a recall of what I had read about these knights and the Crusades in which they had participated.

It must have been more than one hundred years prior to the journey of these nine men that the great armies of the first Crusades had gone overland. They travelled across the Seine valley and the Alps to the land across the Great Sea, as the Mediterranean was then called, to Outremer, the sacred land beyond the sea. The nine middle-aged men led by Hugh de Payen would not have taken such an arduous route. Instead they would have journeyed overland to Venice and there boarded a sailing ship or galley bound for Acre—the city that served as the principle port city for the Holy Land because of its sheltered harbor. Both cities had prospered mightily from the heavy traffic of pilgrims and commerce which had occurred after 1099 when Jerusalem had been recaptured from the Sunnite sect of Muslims, ruled by the Caliphs of Baghdad. (The same sect of Muslims who are very much in the news at the end of the twentieth century!)

I had a puzzling thought. If these nine men had presented themselves to the King of Jerusalem, how then did they become known as "warrior monks" or the "militia of Christ?" Also, why did history record them to be in wealth the equal of Kings? How could all of this happen to nine middle aged men who went to Jerusalem to help some poor pilgrims? My twentieth century mind wondered if they had unearthed some hidden treasure!

The voice speaking harshly reminded me of his presence.

"It was the intervention of the Church and my liege Lord, the Count of Champagne, that brought us fame and riches; not some mysterious digging for the bones of Christ under the floor of the Holy Sepulchre or some devious scheming, as some have alleged."

I was startled. There must be more to this story than I had ever dreamed or imagined!

More forceful now, the spirit continued:

"It was the Count of Champagne that I wrote to after we reached the Holy City who not only joined us in a few years but brought with him one of the great Lords of all time, Charles Fulk, Count of Anjou. These two men arrived with a letter of appreciation from the Bishop of Chartres. We were overwhelmed. So impressed were these lords and the bishops of the Church with the aid we had given the pilgrims and with our efforts to keep the roads free of bandits and others who would hinder them on their journey to the

Holy Place, that they made gifts to us of large tracts of land."

His voice faded; my mind wandered. How did this revelation square with my knowledge that these knights had been sworn to the vow of poverty, obedience and chastity?

The ghostly voice got stronger.

"You interrupt me with your thoughts."

I shivered. He must be able to read my mind!

"I can, so please allow me to continue. One of our original nine, Andre de Montbard, was the uncle of Bernard, the famed Abbot of Clairvaux, the monk who founded the Order of Cistercians, and was the chief spokesman of Christendom. In 1127, nine years after we had arrived in Jerusalem, I, along with Andre and the two Lords, left Jerusalem and returned to the city of my birth, Troyes, in my native Champagne. Our purpose was to attend a synod organized by Bernard. We were overwhelmed at the triumphal reception we received."

He seemed to sigh, remembering. I dared not let my mind wander, afraid of a rebuke. A period of silence followed. I was so pregnant with anticipation I froze in place.

After awhile, as I shifted on the bench I had chosen toward the rear of the church, the ghost continued, his voice now so thin and soft I could barely hear it.

". . . the convocation had been called to confer official status on our group. It was a magnificent assemblage. On one side sat the Cardinal-legate of the Pope, ten bishops, and seven Abbots of great eminence, all friends of Bernard. The secular side was equally impressive. Present were Count Tibald of Champagne and Brie, the Count of Nevers and a delegation of nobles, scholars and masters of canon law, and other learned men. No one but Bernard

could command such an attendance."

I began to think of the work of the great St. Bernard. The ghost was indignant.

"I tire of your mental interruptions."

I noticed a thin sliver of light reflecting from the brass plaque on wall. I turned to see if someone had opened the door but there was no one there. I turned back toward the chancel. No one was there, either!

Then I felt or rather sensed something. It was just the whisper of air brushing by me. A hollow echo said:

"Think on it and come back tomorrow."

For a long time I sat lost in thought. Eliot's words came to me.

> This is the use of memory: For liberation not
> less of love but expanding of love beyond de-
> sire, and so liberation from the future as well as
> the past.

So St. Bernard had been involved with the Knights Templar. The same Bernard who has been described as a combination of Schweitzer, Churchill and Einstein rolled into one. It made good sense, now that I thought about it. Bernard had been concerned about the fate of Christianity in the Holy Land. Also, he had been greatly concerned about the churlishness and low character of "knighthood" in the world of his time. As founder of the Cistercian order of Monks, he had been privy to the desires of several Popes who yearned for a militia of their own.

What did not make sense, though, was that Bernard seemed to be the last man in the world to found an order of "warrior monks." He was sick most of his life with a series of debilitating ailments: migraine headaches; gastritis; hypertension; even an atrophied sense of taste! Plus the fact that within that frail body was a profound thinker and mystic who would appear to be more at home in the cloister of a monastery than jousting with the problems of the world.

But then Bernard was no ordinary mortal nor monk. He was born a nobleman on the border of Champagne and Burgundy. An intensely compulsive man—opinionated and driven—he avoided sleep and gave in only when he was too faint to keep awake. His massive intellect came together in two powerful talents: organizer and writer.

The Council of Troyes, which the ghost of Hugh de Payen had just told me about, had been the handiwork of St. Bernard. Under his coaching from afar (he had been too sick to attend the meeting in person) the convocation officially recognized Hugh's group as a religious—military order with Hugh de Payen as Grand Master. This was the first time the title had ever been conferred. But Bernard did not stop there. He spent days having Hugh recount his experiences in Jerusalem. Following these sessions, Bernard set about writing a set of Rules for the Brotherhood: Sixty two articles that covered dress, behavior, daily routine, religious duties, military requirements, obedience, property, etc. Nothing was left to chance.

The Knights of the Temple of Solomon or Knights Templar as they came to be known, were sworn to the vows of poverty, chastity and obedience. They could cut their beards but not their hair (clean shaven chins were then in vogue). Diet, religious dress and daily life were regulated to conform to religious and military routine. All Knights were required to wear a white mantle on which was displayed an eight-pointed cross.

Bernard did not stop with setting rules for dress or behaviour. The sixty first and sixty second rules reveal the secret behind the enormous wealth and power these Knights with the red cross on their chests would soon achieve throughout Christendom. In an era when rival Popes were appointing rival bishops, and the church itself was riven with strife, the Knights Templar were permitted to accept as members, individuals (or groups) who had been excommunicated from the church. To appreciate the significance of this rule, one needs only remember that this was the time in which rival Popes could and did excommunicate entire villages!

The final rule is perhaps the strangest and yet the most powerful of all. It applied the vow of poverty only to the personal property of the individual Knight. Everything else belonging to a Knight became the property of the Order!

The effect of these last two rules created a stampede of volunteers eager to join. Men flocked to the Order, giving everything from a house to a whole village, an entire harvest, animals, tithes, and so on, *ad infinitum*. Temple Commanderies and branch Preceptories sprang up all over Europe and England—each having its own Master and system of administration.

My ruminations left me exhausted, astounded and puzzled. None of this history could account for the existence of a Templar church in the east midlands of England. A region of small towns and even smaller villages or parishes—but none as tiny as Little Gidding. But then each piece of history I had unearthed about this church had astounded me as surely as it had T. S. Eliot.

I left the church determined to visit the largest and best example of all Templar churches in England—the one located in the Inns of the Court in central London. Also located there is the large Meeting Hall of the Knights which is now used as a communal luncheon hall for lawyers. Although the church is called a Round church it actually has eight sides. The repeated use of eight makes one think it must have some theological significance—a point I filed away for future research. Perhaps the church at Little Gidding would provide an answer.

The London church, as must have been the case with its tiny counterpart in the midlands, had suffered many ups and downs. It had a narrow escape in the Great London Fire of 1666; and on the night of 10 May 1941, four months before Eliot left London, it was grievously burnt from a bombing raid. The restored church contains effigies of several Knights, some of which are quite damaged. In studying the inscriptions of those that were legible—I was able to decipher the name of at least one of the effigies. It was "Roscelyn de Ros" one of the names on the brass plaque! He was one of the first *Patrons* of the church at Little Gidding.

Further, a descriptive booklet of the London church states: "this Round Church was built on the model of the church of the Holy Sepulchre in Jerusalem and was consecrated on 10 February 1185 in honor of the Blessed Mary, by Heraclius, Patriarch of Jerusalem in the presence of Henry II and his court." I recalled that the ghost of Hugh de Payen had told me that it was Heraclius, the Patriarch of Jerusalem, who received his group when they arrived in the Holy City in 1118. Also, that the property at Little Gidding had been given to the Knights in 1185, the same year the Patriarch dedicated the church in London.

The next day I returned to Little Gidding eager to learn more about the tiny church and its relationship to the knights who wore red eight-pointed crosses on their mantles. A phrase in Eliot's poem came to mind.

> . . . And what you thought you came for is only
> a shell, a husk of meaning from which the pur-
> pose breaks only when it is fulfilled if at all. Ei-
> ther you had no purpose or the purpose is be-
> yond the end you figured and is altered in
> fulfillment . . .

I had a clear purpose when I came here but only time, perhaps this day, would alter that purpose or lead me I knew not where.

As I walked around a tombstone that is located above ground in front of the church, I was aware that this time it was a glorious day in May and the hedges were white and filled with the sweet smell of spring; much different from my first visit and in sharp contradiction to an-

ticipating a meeting with a ghost! On entering the church I
glanced around. The sun was streaming through the windows. I wondered if I would be able to see the spirit of
Hugh de Payen more distinctly? I saw nothing but an empty
church. I heard nothing but the sounds of spring: birds gaily
chattering to one another; distant sounds of workers in the
fields. It was just not the day to talk with ghosts. Just then a
cloud must have momentarily obscured the sun. The church
darkened. One window shone brighter than the rest. I studied the window. It was the southeast Nave window and
known as the King's Window. Then I heard Hugh's voice. It
had an altogether different quality than it had had yester-
day: stronger, more authoritative. Yes, it now sounded like
the voice of one who would lead an Order of Knights that
would survive for two hundred years!
 I caught him in the middle of a sentence:

 *". . . it is very fitting that this window be known as
the King's Window even though it was meant to commemorate a King who was succored by this church long after I
departed the world."*

 The voice's next statement caught me off guard. It
was a question!

 *"Have you thought of my admonition when I left you
yester-morn?"*

 "You mean . . . ?"

 I stammered, not able to quickly recall; so much
was happening to me.

 *"Yes, . . . for you to stop interrupting me by silent
thoughts which you engage in while I speak. Do you
agree?"*

 Again that tone of authority. I nodded, almost

dumbly.

Hugh continued:

"Several years after the Council of Troyes; years when Temple Commanderies and Preceptories were springing up in the south of France and in Spain but not in Portugal because the Moorish flood was at high tide there, I came to England at the behest of King Henry II. I was received with honor and given gifts of gold and silver for the benefit of the Order. His Royal Highness was enthusiastic about the new Knighthood and gave great assistance in recruiting Knights. Temple Commanderies were formed first in London, and then in Lincolnshire, Essex, Buckinghamshire, Hertfordshire and elsewhere. Large landholders such as the Engayne family here in the east midlands gave or sold land for a mere pittance to be used as Preceptories—the smaller religious houses of our Order."

"I have before told you that Charles, Count of Anjou, was a member of my original group in the Holy Land. Have I not?"

"Yes," I answered, almost subserviently, not wishing to offend.

"Charles," he continued, *"was the King's grandfather. It was for this reason that later on our Order would give every assistance to King Henry in his difficulties with Thomas a' Becket. But to no avail. The Archbishop was murdered."*

I was aware that the Archbishop had been murdered but I did not know the Knights had tried to help.

"Then you should know," Hugh went on, *"the Order was deeply involved in the affairs of England for many*

years. Following the reign of King Henry II, his brother, Richard I, virtually ignored his royal position by joining the Third Crusade and spending most of his life in the Holy Land away from England. By the time John, Henry II's youngest son, became King, the Grand Masters of the Knights Templar in England were regularly called to Parliament and were considered as ecclesiastical barons."

"The King considered the Temple Commandery in London to be the safest place in England during his fight with the barons. Indeed, he had the Grand Master, Aymeric de St. Maur, at his right hand when facing the barons on the fields of Runnymede. Aymeric's signature is on the document you now call the 'Magna Carta.'"

Heady stuff this, I thought, but how does it all fit in with this tiny church and village?

Hugh's voice became almost wistful as he answered my question.

"Temple Bruer to which Gidding Engayne was attached played two important roles in the Order. But first, you must understand, that recruits were accepted into the Order with the following prayer: 'In the name of God and Our Lady Mary and in the name of all brethren of the Temple, we accept you, your Mother, and all your family whom you wish to participate therein, as sharing the good works of the Order since its foundation and such shall be done until the end.' Thus, a Preceptory became the home—a sanctuary, if you please—for the Knight's family, if he and they so chose, while he was abroad."

"Secondly, when the aged Templar had outlived his usefulness, loving provision was made . . . and special houses were maintained in the West. Little Gidding was early on a commune for the Knight's family when he was young and a place of refuge when he was old."

The last statement was made so softly it made me feel that Hugh was getting tired. I recalled Eliot's conversation with his ghost:

> ". . . He left me, with a kind of valediction, and
> faded on the blowing of the horn . . . "

I looked up at the window. The glow was gone and so was Hugh. In the distance I heard the whistle of the afternoon train to London.

Left alone, I ruminated about the history of Knights Templar as I knew it. Hugh de Payen died on May 26, and was succeeded by Robert de Craon, whom legend has it was a relative of the Archbishop of Canterbury. While my visitor, 'Hugh,' seems to have been a good organizer he was not much of a thinker or politician. Robert, on the other hand, was a masterful schemer. In swift succession, he took several fateful actions. First, he extended associate status in the Knights Templar to women of an age not to give rise to temptation nor evil gossip, who upon the cessation of their lives would leave their fortunes to the Order. When the Pope heard of this action, he issued a long, detailed letter emancipating the Templars from all ecclesiastical or temporal authority, except his own. Further, the Pontiff exempted them from having to pay tithes (taxes); granted them exclusive rights over all tithes made to them; made all of their deliberations and activities in their commanderies private (secret). In return, the Knights were to swear they would not rub shoulders with sinful persons or frequenters of women!

Second, the new Grand Master persuaded the King of Aragon, upon his death, to donate one-third of his entire kingdom to the Order of the Temple. However, when the King died, his heirs contested the Royal Will and Robert, with enormous foresight that would contribute to the good fortune of the future of the Order, gracefully waived the Order's share of the estate.

Over time, the Knights Templar prospered, militarily as well as financially. They became the most disciplined fighting force in the Crusades. Recruits from all over Europe rushed to join the Order. Temple Commanderies and smaller Preceptories spread across the entire route to the Holy Land. The Masters of these Commanderies successfully engaged in diplomacy, political intrigue and last but not least, finance. Most scholars of the Order of the Temple maintain that the Commanderies served as transfer points for money moving in both directions. Also, that such modern financial instruments as the bank check and the letter of credit were invented by the Templars. Further, that the Temple in Paris, as one example, became the center of emerging European commerce and that the King of France called it the safest depository in the world. The Order it seemed had strayed a long way from its simple but noble beginning.

After a time, I got up and looked at the brass plaque. The next two entries read:

1335 - Cessation
1335 - Bishop of Lincoln, Patron

Strange—two events happening in one year! I looked toward the KING'S window hoping Hugh de Payen would return and enlighten me. Nothing. I looked across the Nave at another window known as the BISHOP'S window. The text above it paraphrased a passage from St.Paul's Letter to Titus: " . . . Bishops should be 'not grasping but hospitable. . . ' "

Well, I thought to myself, apparently the prelate had not just come in and seized the place. Just the thought made me feel better. At least the poor families and pensioners who must have lived here were not just summarily removed.

"Not at all," a firm, authoritative voice said.

I jumped in fright, and spun around. No one was in

the church. The voice was so clear and present I thought someone had come up behind me.

"If you will go sit opposite that brass plaque I'll explain," the voice ordered me.

I promptly did as I was told. As I did so, I became aware that the window I had been looking at, the northeast Nave window to the right of the brass plaque, now had that same unnatural glow I'd noticed when Hugh de Payen paid me a second visit. This time, though, the voice did not provide any identification. The positive strength of the voice just suggested I should know who was speaking. It had the timbre of a trained speaker; a clergyman, I guessed.

"That plaque is still not accurate in one respect. The Templars ceased to exist in Europe in 1312 but, because of the haggling that went on in England, they held onto this property until 1335 when it ceased to be a Templar property and later in the year was placed under my juridiction."

I decided to be bold.

"Were the families of the Templars and the pensioners removed or hurt in any way at that time? Was there an uprising of some sort?" I asked.

"No, not here. Not anywhere in England."

I persisted.

"I'm just curious about what happened to the Knights Templar and to this church that would cause its cessation."

"My dear fellow, that word belongs to those who

made the plaque but it has nothing to do with the status of this church. The church and the community of families of the knights and the pensioners went on as before, but under my auspices as Patron and then only for a few months."

"May I be so bold as to inquire what happened to the Knights?"

The voice answered matter of factly,

"Over time they were destroyed, mostly in France but finally here in England, too."

"But they were so powerful, wealthy and so highly thought of, that hardly seems possible," I protested.

The voice sounding very ecclesiastical responded.

"People do not like to be humiliated, especially Kings! But even Kings find they cannot act except when the power of the Holy See is behind them. If you will please not interrupt me I will attempt to make you understand."

I sat quiet as a mouse in a church.

"The Holy Wars to rescue the Lord's Sepulchre from the hand of the Muslims took place during the years the Church was growing in power throughout the world. Those who took up the Cross—known as Crusaders— fought valiantly and their failure was in no way due to the leadership of St. Bernard and the several Popes who gave their blessing. But when King Frederick II of Sicily and his recently formed Teutonic Knights attempted to make a separate truce with the Muslims, over the vigorous objections of Pope Gregory IX, trouble began. The truce proved to be an illusion and a sham. Within a few years both Jerusalem

and Acre, the main port city for the Holy Land, were taken by Islam. This was a disaster for the Knights Templar who were forced to flee. At that time many people believed the reason for their existence had ceased."

It was on the tip of my tongue to ask a question at this point but I knew I dare not.

"... However, by the time this happened the Knights were established in every country in Christendom. In France, to the consternation of the reigning monarch, Philip IV, known as Philip, the Fair, because of his light complexion, they had become the wealthiest and most powerful group in his kingdom."

"Philip, tall, handsome, and unseemly arrogant, held not one but two grudges against them. At one time, he made a thinly disguised effort to gain control of the Knights Templar by becoming a 'postulant' or beginning member. This was quickly detected by their Grand Master and Philip was rejected! Later, when the people of France rioted against his purchase tax on all commodities, the 'Maltote' as the hated levy was called, Philip was forced to seek refuge from the mob in the Temple in Paris. Instead of feeling gratitude toward the Templars, he felt humiliated. His hurt was not even assuaged when due to his financial condition the Knights paid his daughter's dowry."

"By the year 1306, Philip's humiliation was fueled by two other factors: he owed the Templars a great deal of money, and he was terrified that they might plan to make France their permanent home—perhaps even an independent state within his kingdom. He decided to act."

I could not contain myself any longer so I blurted out, forgetting the situation I was in,

"But according to what I now know of the Knights

Templar, the only power on earth to whom they owed allegiance was the Pope. How could the King of France as powerful as he might be, do them any harm?"

Silence.

I started to say something more but held back fearing I had angered the spirit whom I had guessed must be the Bishop of Lincoln. Apparently I had. The silence continued. I looked steadily at the window hoping that my strict attention might gain me some favor. Silence. After awhile I noticed the glow from the Bishop's window fading. Oh no, I thought, don't leave me now just when I was beginning to understand what might have happened to the Knights Templar. Finally, I left the church and decided to continue my research at the Library of the British Museum, one of most famous libraries in the world.

The more familiar I became with the routine of ordinary life in a Temple Commandery (and even more so in a Preceptory such as Little Gidding) the more puzzled I became. The daily regime and the variety of duties performed were strikingly familiar to those of a monastery. Carpenters, smithies, shepherds, gardeners, cooks, masons, dairymen, bookkeepers and more were among the skills and crafts needed to make this a self-sufficient Preceptory.

A typical day was to rise before dawn, to hear the Matins and do the morning chores. Breakfast was bread and coffee; lunch a meatless meal, accompanied by reading and silence. In the afternoon, everyone assembled for Vespers, followed by supper. Before retiring for the night, everyone assembled for an evening service after which orders for the next day were issued.

This peaceful, tranquil, monastic setting seemed to explain very clearly the life of the Templars who lived at Little Gidding but it certainly was in stark contrast to the historical Templars who are depicted in most of the literature as the most colorful, powerful and well known of all the crusaders.

Since the Bishop of Lincoln had left me in the middle of a muddle about the relationship of the Order to the King of France, I decided to visit a friend of mine who lived part of the year in Paris and part in the south of France. She had always seemed to know everything about 'la belle Francaise.' To my amazement, when I briefly informed her what I was about and asked her about the Knights Templar, she stared at me and replied, "That is not a subject that is talked much about in France!"

Later on in my visit, however, I discovered that Paris bookstores were filled with histories of the Order: some straight forward, others bordered on the ridiculous, suggesting the Templars dealt in such esoteric and weird subjects as alchemy, astrology, sacred geometry and even wild tales about skulls and bones. No wonder my French friend refused to discuss the subject. By vocation she was an artist but underneath she was a very practical business woman.

I decided to return to England and visit a small library maintained by the modern Order of St. John, located in Clerkenwell, a section of London not far from the British Museum. It contained substantial documentation relating to the demise of the Knights Templars. The story is filled with as much intrigue as is found in any good adventure novel.

My question as to how the French King could act without the support of the Pope now took on greater meaning. The Pope at the time Philip decided to take action against the Knights Templar was Pope Boniface VIII, an Italian, who had large ambitions of his own that were directly contradictory, not only to the King of France but to every King. It was Boniface's intention to seize greater power over all Kings, especially those not of his own blood. To achieve his purpose, the Pope issued a Papal Bull (letter) proclaiming the inferiority of all Kings to the Pope.

This was too much for Philip. In a series of actions worthy of a Hitler or a Stalin in the 20th century, Philip undertook to destroy not only Boniface, but his successor, Pope Benedict XI. He did so in a very modern way; he used secret agents. It is hard to find amusement in such sinister undertakings, but the name of Philip's chief secret agent offers a bit of comic relief—his name, not his personality or methods—it being William de Nogaret: William, the Nut!

A lawyer and a skilled politician, William was able to turn Boniface's Bull against the Papacy itself. He formed a coalition of Lords, arguing that the Pope's action threatened all nobility. In due course, an insurrection was mounted against Boniface while he was in residence in the small Italian town of Agnani. During the rioting, the Pope was seized, held in confinement and died, reportedly of a kidney disease. When Benedict XI, became Pope, he proved no more amenable to Philip's ideas than his predecessor. So in a short time he, too, became seriously ill and died of an unknown cause. Philip, now tiring of Italian Popes, decided to name his own Vicar of Christ. He chose a Frenchman, the Archbishop of Bordeaux, as successor to Benedict. Claiming that unrest in Rome placed the Papacy in danger, Philip installed Clement V, with appropriate ceremony, at Lyon, France. He then had the Holy See moved to the city of Avignon, in the south of France.

In a series of breathtaking actions, the new Pope named ten new Cardinals: nine French and one English; he conferred many benefits upon the French King, including review of drafts of all Papal Bulls (scrutinized and edited no doubt by William, the Nut)!

Philip was now prepared to deliver the *coup de grace* to the Knights Templar. But to his chagrin, Clement V, proved reluctant. After all, the Knights were, among other things, financiers of the Papacy. But, treasure not withstanding, their overweening arrogance finally did them in. When Clement, possibly at William, the Nut's suggestion, sought to bring them under tighter control by naming a member of his inner circle as their overseer; they flatly refused. Clement could not long tolerate their intransigence. He was so beholden to Philip that he finally capitulated and Philip and his agent, William, the Nut, acted without delay. In the classic moves of the modern dictator, the King had a list of charges drawn up; infiltrated the Order with his spies; wrung "voluntary" confessions from these spurious

"Knights," and finally, on October 13, 1307, in a move that chillingly recalls the actions of the Gestapo, all *les Templiers*, as the Knights Templar are called by French historians, were seized, their goods confiscated, and they were hauled off to jail to be tormented and tortured. The Knights were forced to admit they worshipped a devil called Baphomet; prostrated themselves before a bearded skull; and even that-they repudiated Christ and spat upon the Cross. (I finally realized what my first visitor, Hugh de Payen, meant when he referred to the dastardly things the Templars were accused of doing.)

Strange to report, though, the swift, silent, deadly actions of Philip's minions failed to uncover the secret treasure of the Templars—nor has it been found to this day. The content of that treasure has inspired many authors of both fiction and non-fiction: some claim it contains the birth records of Jesus; others maintain it is the testament of Judas Iscariot. All the researchers of the Templars seem to agree that whatever the secret is it is located somewhere in the south of France. But even stranger tales were yet to come.

In 1312, Philip's brother, Valois, convened the Council of Vienne. The purpose of the Council was officially to abolish the Knights Templar (at least in France). On March 18, 1314, Jacques de Molay and other leaders of the Order were put to death at the pyre. To all intents and purposes the Order ceased to exist. But other monarchs were not so eager to follow Philip.

In England, Philip's own son-in-law, Edward II, at first rallied to their defense. But again, the Pope stepped in. Clement V, had extracted a price from Philip for his part in the destruction of the Order: all of their properties were to be turned over to the Knights Hospitalers of St. John of Jerusalem, an Order of Knights which had agreed to come under the complete control and direction of the Papacy, even to having their Grand Master (later changed to Grand Prior) appointed by His Holiness.

The King of England resisted for some years. When

he gave in, he seldom did more than order the knights to do penance in an abbey or a monastery. But confiscating their property was another matter and all the thundering of the Pope was to no avail. For fifteen years, Edward, assisted by the powerful barons, held off the Pope and his bishops in England. Finally, he was forced to abdicate and was murdered in Berkeley Castle (where, it is said, his ghost is alleged to appear with some regularity). Historians attribute his demise to the actions of his wife, Isabella, who by coincidence happened to be Philip's daughter.

Legend has it that the last words spoken by Jacques de Molay, the Grand Master of all Knights Templar, just before he succumbed to the flames, placed a curse on his accusers and tormentors. Be that as it may, history reveals that Philip died a month almost to the day after Jacques; Clement V, died nine months later; and William, the Nut, died before the year was out.

But the story of the Knights Templar in England was not over. Edward's successor, King Edward III, of the House of Windsor, tried for several years not to interfere with the right of the Templars to their property. His lack of action enjoyed popular support primarily because when all the charges against them were closely examined the main one appeared to be heresy, and not even all the clerics, under whose aegis such a charge was supposed to fall, were convinced of their guilt. No less an ecclesiastical leader than the Archbishop of York was included among the doubters.

In due time, however, the Pope and the Bishops who supported his stand succeeded in obtaining an act of Parliament transferring all the properties of the Knights Templar to the Knights Hospitalers of St. John of Jerusalem. Still the Templars refused to budge. Finally, in 1334, a fresh act of Parliament was passed, confirming the original act and empowering the sheriffs to take possession of all Templar properties, except for the Temple in London which was transferred in 1340. Undoubtedly, the Bishop of Lincoln had been an active participant in lobbying Parliament and was quite aware of the feeling among the people of England concerning the Templars. Hence, the unwillingness of his spirit to discuss the subject.

From the information I had garnered from my research it was apparent that a new chapter in the life of the church at Little Gidding was about to unfold, so I hurried there. As I entered the church I went straignt to the brass plaque. The entry surprised me. It was the third one shown for the year 1335, and was listed just below the one for the Bishop of Lincoln. It read:

1335—Philip de Thame, Prior, Hospitalers of St. John of Jerusalem, Patron

Apparently, the process used in transferring the property of the Knights Templar in England had three stages. First, it was taken from the Knights (Cessation). Second, it was transferred to the jurisdiction of the diocese headed by a Bishop. Third, it was transferred to another organization of Knights. But who were these Hospitalers of the Order of St. John and why had the property been turned over to them so promptly?

I stared at the eight-pointed crosses on the font.

"I can give the answer to those questions," a strong, powerful, authoritative voice behind me said.

I turned quickly. Standing in front of the brass plaque was a short, erect figure clothed in a black robe on the left breast of which was a white eight-pointed cross. His eyes were opaque and I thought he wore a beard but I could not be sure. It was hard to describe him—he seemed transparent—yet his presence was intimidating. I had learned my lesson from the experience with the Bishop so I held my tongue as well as my breath.

He continued.

"Allow me to introduce myself. My name is Philip de Thame, Grand Prior of the Hospitalers of St. John in

England, under whose administration the Order took possession of all Templar properties, including Little Gidding.
You will notice I wear on my mantle over my left breast the
cross with the eight points. It is the symbol of our Order
and was selected by Pope Paschal II many years before the
Order of the Temple was founded .... "

I wanted to ask why it was white and not red like
the Templars cross but I kept silent.

He continued, but changed the subject by asking a
question which puzzled me more than the one I had just
thought about but I held my tongue.

"It almost seems that our inheritance of these properties brought a curse with it, doesn't it?"

What did he mean?

"Awful things were about to happen in this area; to
England and to all of Europe for that matter," he paused
for a moment seemingly lost in thought. Then he continued,
"At the time we took over these properties the throne was
occupied by a boy of fourteen, Edward III, whose uncle,
John of Gaunt, was the Regent of England. John and his
Ministers in an effort to raise funds invented a Poll Tax, a
flat rate of four pence on every adult in the country. The tax
hit the poor harder than the rich. Four pence a head was
harder on the farm laborer than on the merchant in London. As the new Patrons of the Commanderies and Preceptories in England, we were required to collect the tax. Here
at Little Gidding, as elsewhere, we were met with an intense and frightening hostility among the peasants in the
surrounding areas."

"However, that situation ended in a most terrifying
manner, the like of which had never before been seen in
this world. The black plague arrived in England and the re-

gion surrounding Little Gidding was not spared from this most terrible of all terrors. Peasants from the surrounding countryside began to appear at the entrance to the Preceptory with strange swellings about the size of an egg in their armpits and groins. The swellings began to ooze blood and were followed by spreading boils and black blotches on the skin. Very quickly they began coughing and spitting blood. None of us had ever seen anything like it in our entire lives. We did everything we could to help these poor people but nothing worked. Even the physicians were of no help; they had not the slightest idea what was causing the dread disease. Soon high fever followed and although we did everything we knew to aid them, they died within three days or less. Then people from all over the region began crowding the church believing the scourge was a kind of Divine punishment for their sins. The loud imprecations to God emanating from the church now joined the moaning and crying of the suffering of the sick and dying who covered every square inch of the Preceptory: manor house; the church; adjacent buildings; even the roads. It was like a scene from hell."

I was so horror stricken I just sat staring at the apparition in the black robe with the white eight-pointed cross. He seemed not to pay any attention to me. After a while I was tempted to ask him what happened to the church and the village but I knew I dare not. As before, he knew my innermost thoughts. Scary.

Solemnly, he continued.

"The church survived, although just barely. In every age no matter what befalls man, God keeps coming on. But the village was decimated. The Preceptory had some 31 households before the plague; aferwards there were six left. Six hundred acres had been under cultivation; afterwards no more than 20 were worked. As a result of the

sickness, this community, as did many others, gave up farming and turned to livestock raising—it required much less human labor. Sheep raising now became the major activity of the region."

"Forgive me for getting ahead of my story. I must have gotten carried away by the memories of the terrors which occurred just after we took over this and other properties of the Templars . . . and for many years to follow . . ."

The spirit of Philip de Thame sighed such a deep sigh, I felt embarrassed. It must have been a terribly hurtful memory.

After awhile, he continued.

"I am aware that you have been searching out the background of the Patrons of this church. Our Order started in a hospital. In the year 1023 certain merchants of Amalfi, a town in Italy, obtained permission from the Caliph of Egypt to establish a hospital in Jerusalem for the use of poor and sick Latin pilgrims to the Holy Land. It soon prospered and word of its fame spread throughout Europe. Grateful travellers sent offerings of funds; others voluntarily remained behind to assist in its pious purposes."

"When Godfrey de Bouillon took Jerusalem from the infidels, his wounded crusaders were tended by Peter Gerard, the rector of the hospital, known as the Hospital of St. John. With Jerusalem once again in the hands of Christian forces, pilgrims now came to the city in greater numbers. This placed a great burden upon the facilites of the hospice and better organization became imperative. In turn, this led to the origin of the Knight Hospitalers of St. John of Jerusalem."

The voice of Philip de Thame had gotten softer and softer and now stopped altogether. I sat quietly not know-

ing what I should do. Most certainly, I would not interrupt
nor in any manner interfere with his fascinating recitation.
He continued. His voice regained strength.

*"It was Peter Gerard who proposed that a regularly
constituted religious body be formed. The Patriarch of Jerusalem agreed and invested every approved candidate
with a black robe bearing on the breast an eight-pointed
white cross. The eight points were symbolic of the eight different languages represented in the new Order. However,
they had a higher and more important meaning; they were
intended to symbolize the eight beatitudes in the Holy
Scriptures. Thus, the cross is worn on the breast over the
heart to remind each Knight that he should cherish these
virtues and never desert them or lay them aside."*

The meaning of what Philip de Thame had just told
me lay heavily on my heart. I had known this was really a
noble order of Knighthood but I was not aware of the reason behind their devoted service to the poor and the sick,
and their stalwart defense of Christianity. With this in
mind, I decided to question him further.

*"I have noticed the eight-pointed crosses on the
baptismal font of this church but I did not know the meaning of the eight-points. For that matter, I was not until now
aware of the reason the buildings of your order and those
of the Templars had eight sides. Now I know. But I had
read that the crosses were called Maltese crosses. Why are
they given that name?"*

Philip answered.

*"In time, Peter Gerard felt he should attend to his
hospital duties and he was succeeded by Raymond de Puy.
It was he who caused the monastic Hospitalers to under-
take a fresh oath to become militant defenders of the faith.*

After a troubled existence in the Holy Land, the Order was compelled to evacuate Palestine, and over time move from island to island in the Great Sea, which you now call the Mediterranean. Finally, in 1530, the Knights were given the island of Malta to have as their headquarters. From that time on the eight-pointed cross became known as the Maltese Cross."

I nodded my thanks for this new knowledge but I had another question burning in my head.

The ghost of Philip de Thame immediately read my mind.

"What is it you now want to know?"

I pointed to the words over the chancel:

O FOR THE PEACE OF JERUSALEM.

"What is the meaning of those words and why is there an eight-pointed cross on either side of them?" I asked.

Philip de Thame was quiet for a moment as he studied the legend. Then he answered, slowly.

"It has great and solemn meaning to all Knights and it always will. Ever since King David brought the Ark of the Covenant to Jerusalem it has been a holy city. A city revered by Jews and Christian alike. Indeed, the 122nd Psalm prays that Jerusalem will be restored and made whole again. The Knights of St. John used this phrase as their rule and guide in trying to wrest Jerusalem from the infidels so it is fitting that in this sanctuary the motto and symbol of our Order is preserved. I doubt that you will ever find it such anywhere in the entire world. But alas, alas,

even to this day, there is still no peace in Jerusalem."

The silence in the small church was as still as a tomb. I sat quietly staring at the legend over the chancel. When I turned to look at the ghost of Philip de Thame, he was no longer there. I looked at the brass plaque and saw the frightening but now familiar words:

1540 - Cessation.

2

THE CROWN AND THE CROSS

The strange entry on the brass plaque was puzzling. There is evidence that neither the church nor the Knights disappeared. To this day, the Knights of St. John exist in England, the United States and Rome. The head of the Order in the Vatican is second in command to the Pope—a position that had been created when the Knights Templar were destroyed.

The middle of the sixteenth century, though, was a period of great turmoil in England and Little Gidding was in no way immune from it. Indeed, the church and the Knights were very much involved in the upheaval. Because the Order was not responsible to any temporal authority it followed that everything they owned in England belonged to the Papacy. It has been established with a degree of certainty if anything in history can really ever be described as certain—that the community of Little Gidding was a monastic setting of sorts providing succor to families of all knights and to those who had retired from active service. In its daily routines, it followed the procedures and devotionals of a fairly typical monastery. In April, 1536, Little Gidding for all intents and purposes was a vibrant, albeit small, functioning monastery. Except for its diminutive size it was not unlike hundreds of other religious houses, monasteries, nunneries and friaries spread throughout England. In total, they controlled almost a third of the land in England. All of which was owned by the Papacy in Rome and to which all "annates"—ten percent of all income, went to the Pope. Close to ten thousand knights, monks, nuns, and friars, occupied these lands.

By April, 1540, the year listed on the brass plaque, all of these properties had been taken over by the crown and all but a few had been leased or sold to lay occupiers. It appears that a few were held in the possession of the crown; others were cathedral abbeys and not involved in the dissolution.

Was such disruption necessary? Had the Knight Hospitalers of the Order of St. John grown so powerful that they brought down the ire of a King upon their heads as had the Knights Templar? Was Little Gidding once again victimized by matters far beyond its ken? The answers to those questions proved complex, and quite unreal. I hoped a ghost would come forth and provide me with the insights needed to understand yet another riddle about this strange and wonderful place. None appeared so I was left to my own devices.

It appears that over a period of time people in the surrounding areas developed suspicions about the cloistered life of the monks and nuns who lived in the community. Yes, and they were even suspicious about the elderly Knights and their families. Suspicion is not an unnatural reaction when a community is cut off from normal intercourse with its neighbors; a condition that would come to haunt Little Gidding in later years. The suspicions and criticisms that resulted from this lack of communication inevitably led to charges of immoral conduct. After all, the standards of moral conduct are set by the community and if a group, any group, closets itself off so to speak, the natural human response, whether we agree with it or not, is to assert that something not moral must be occurring in the closet. That is what happened to the monasteries, nunneries and preceptories of the Knights in medieval England.

The accusations against these communities covered the entire spectrum of sexual promiscuity: pregnant nuns were whispered about; homosexuality was considered commonplace; abuse of young children was rife, and so on. The records show that in 1536, four years before the fateful entry on the brass plaque at Little Gidding, the Pope's leading

Prelate in England, Cardinal Wolsey, had ordered his secretary, a certain Thomas Cromwell, to investigate these accusations and report to him. The letters from Cromwell's agents that still survive present a scandalous picture, indeed.

According to these reports, breaches of the vows of chastity were commonplace in the smaller religious houses; loose discipline was evident; neglect of ritual was widespread and, in general, the moral turpitude left much to be desired. Whether all or any of this is fact or fancy is difficult to assess because Cardinal Wolsey had, according to a Bishop of the Church at the time, risen to such an exalted status, at least in his own eyes as well as in those of King and Pope, that he could comment to Cromwell that he had almost grown to distrust and despise even the ordinary clergy who served under him. One can only wonder if the Cardinal and his secretary were reporting the truth or engaging in confirming their own prejudices. Be that as it may, the report paved the way for the eventual suppression and dissolution of all monasteries in 1540—and Little Gidding was no exception. But as we have learned, repeatedly, nothing about this place is ever as it seems to be, or as Eliot expresses it,

> . . . We shall not cease from exploration.
> And the end of all our exploring
> will be to arrive where we started
> and know the place for the first time.

So there is more to the story than first meets the eye. In fact, the events leading up to the entry on the plaque have all the ingredients of grand opera, and would be entertaining but for their dire consequences. The Monarchy and the Papacy were involved, two from each! One Pope was Julius II, the other, Clement VII. The Kings were father and son, Henry VII and Henry VIII of England.

Although no William, the Nut, came forth to enter the fray there were plenty of characters involved whose actions were just as devious and erratic. Many of the elements of the prior disputes between the crown and church were present this time: money, power, and spurious charges. But two new ones were added: religion and sex.

Henry VII was in such need of money that he married off his eldest son, the Prince of Wales, a lad of fourteen named Arthur, to a Spanish noblewoman named, Catherine, for her dowry. It was said to be worth several hundred thousand pounds. After they had been married for only five months, Arthur died. He had just turned fifteen. In a spurious effort to retain the enormous dowry, Henry 'arranged' with the Spanish Ambassador to send Catherine's father, the King of Spain (or Aragon as it was then known) 'proof' that the marriage had been consummated. To Henry's consternation, Catherine denied that such had not been the case and her father believed her.

But Henry would not be denied the dowry. He now made his second son, also named Henry, the Prince of Wales, and proposed he wed Arthur's widow. At this point the Bible and a Pope entered the picture. Church officials pointed out to the King that a passage in the Old Testament: Leviticus 20:21, made such a union impossible. The passage reads: "If a man shall take his brother's wife it is an unclean thing . . . and they shall be childless . . . . "

The point was vital since it meant that no heir to the throne of England could be produced from such a marriage. However, other church leaders soon came forth and called attention to another passage in the Holy Scriptures that contradicted the Book of Leviticus. According to their reading of the Scriptures, Deuteronomy 25:5, addressed the issue head on and made the proposed marriage entirely correct. The passage states: "If brethren dwell together, and one of them die, and have no child . . . her husband's brother shall take her to him to wife. . . ."

This seemed to clear up the matter, but the Pope at the time was Julius II. He had serious, personal misgivings about the marriage, and the conflicting advice he was receiving from high churchmen in England and Rome did not allay his concerns. After a great deal of hesitation, he finally made up his mind that the passage from Deuteronomy applied to the marriage in question. Forthwith, the couple was granted the necessary Papal dispensation to marry. But Henry, the groom-to-be, was only twelve at the time so cohabitation had to be postponed.

Soon, the youth himself began to have doubts about marrying the older woman—she was twenty-one. Two years later, at age fourteen, he asked to be released from making any commitment to her. His father, King Henry VII, was adamant about the dowry and prevailed on his son to change his mind "in the interests of England." Four years later the father died and, at the age of eighteen, the youth became Henry VIII, King of England. Six weeks after his accession to the throne he acquiesced and publicly celebrated his marriage to Catherine.

Whether because of her own genetic structure, or Henry's, (the Tudor line had a notorious history of fetal problems), Catherine had a terrible time with her pregnancies. Within seven months her first child died at birth; a year later a male baby died within two weeks; as did another and yet another. Henry, never wild about the marriage to the older woman, was now certain he had made a mistake. He harbored thoughts of having the marriage declared invalid using the biblical interpretation given in the passage from the Book of Leviticus. But to his surprise, within a year, Catherine brought a baby to term; a daughter and named her Mary. Henry now believed it was possible a boychild would follow and decided to continue with the marriage.

Two years passed and, alas, Catherine had another stillbirth. But Henry's impetuousness had created a new complication. Shortly after Mary was born, The King, believing as he did that a son would soon follow, betrothed his infant daughter, Mary, aged two, to the dauphin of France. He did so in the belief it would strengthen his Kingdom in its relations with the French. Now, faced with another stillbirth by Catherine he realized that if his daughter, Mary, were to inherit the throne of England, her husband would become the King of both England and France.

In such event, England would become merely a province of France. Panic set in.

Henry now took the position that the reason God did not grant him a son was simply Divine Punishment. Pope Julius, Henry reasoned, and not the King of England, had violated Holy Scripture by authorizing his first marriage to Catherine! Forthwith, he lost interest in Catherine and her child, and did everything possible to distance himself from them and to make their lives as miserable as possible.

By now a viral man of thirty-four, the King followed two separate paths to secure a male heir to the throne. First, he allowed his sexual desires free rein and consorted with one eligible female after another. A strange unwritten law of royalty—probably devised by them—maintained that if a King married for affairs of state, he was permitted to engage in romance outside of the conjugal bed. Henry pursued this law with vigor. Second, he pursued a woman who appealed to him as a possible wife and opened the issue of having his marriage annulled. This time around, his position was supported by the leading Papal Legate in England, none other than Cardinal Wolsey.

Clement VII, had succeeded Pope Julius, and he was reluctant to admit that his predecessor had committed an error in interpreting Holy Scripture when he approved Henry's marriage to Catherine. But there was more to the Pope's stance than met the eye.

Catherine's brother, Charles, was now the King of Spain and Clement was mortally afraid of him. In fact, the Papacy at the time was virtually captive to the Spanish Emperor so the Pope vacillated on the entire issue. An impatient and impulsive man, Henry became disgusted with the Holy See and proceeded forthwith to divorce Catherine and marry the girl he had taken to his bed. Her name was Anne Boleyn.

At the same time, he maneuvered the Parliament and the Convocation of Bishops to make the Catholic Church in England an arm of the state and independent of Rome. To his chagrin, after all of this politicking, and perhaps secretly hoping the Pope would relent and approve both his divorce from Catherine and marriage to Anne, his new wife presented him with another girl, named Elizabeth. Henry had set up a new Church of England; had been excommunicated by the Pope for doing so, and had two daughters and no son.

In the affairs of state, Henry was aided by the same man who had earlier helped Cardinal Wolsey bring in the report of alleged scandalous hehavior in the monasteries, Thomas Cromwell. A manipulator par excellence, Cromwell had made a fortune in both textiles and money-lending before becoming Secretary to the Cardinal. It was Cromwell who now made a suggestion that captured the King's imagination: Parliament should pass an Act of Suppression that would declare Henry's marriage to Catherine invalid; her female child, Mary, a bastard; and Elizabeth heir to the Crown unless Anne begat a male child. Further, all Englishmen and women: monks, nuns, priests, everyone, would be required to take an oath of loyalty to the King.

Henry, although dubious at making a female, any female, heir to the throne of England since he considered most females rather imbecilic, was enthralled with Cromwell's idea and not only persuaded Parliament to pass the Act of Suppression but had them embellish it by making him sovereign over both church and state in England; christen the new church "Ecclesia Anglicana;" and give the King complete power over morals, heresy, creed and ecclesiastical reform—this last to extend to Bishops of the Church requiring them to swear never to consent to resumption of papal authority in England. In fact, if not in title, Henry now became Pope of the Church of England!

Even though he achieved what just a few short years before would have been considered unachieveable, Henry was still not satisfied: politically, familywise, sexually. When Anne Boleyn, to his great dismay, delivered him of another dead baby on the very day that his first wife, Catherine of Aragon was buried, he decided to get another wife!

This time it was one of Anne's maids, Jane Seymour. In an effort to avoid trouble with the Holy See, Henry now acted, undoubtedly with the help of Thomas Cromwell, to dispose of his second Queen, Anne Boleyn. This he did by having her accused of adultery and sent to the Tower of London to lose her head. Within days of her death and just five months after Catherine's, Henry married Jane Seymour and proclaimed her Queen.

Again, the astute Cromwell made the necessary political arrangements. On his advice Henry sought and received from Parliament a new Act of Succession. By this act both Elizabeth and Mary were declared illegimate, and the crown was settled on the prospective issue of the new Queen who history records was a descendant of Edward, III.

Finally, all of this torturous ecclesiastical, political and sexual maneuvering paid off: On October 12, 1537, a male heir was born. All England rejoiced in the birth of Edward VI, the next and future King of England. Poor Jane, however, died some twelve days after he was born.

By the year, 1540, Henry felt he had solved the problem of obtaining a male heir to succeed him (and not incidently removing the threat occasioned by Mary's betrothal as an infant to the dauphin of France) and moved on to political matters. He was now the most absolute monarch England had ever known but he was also absolutely broke. His personal and court expenses were beyond belief; he wanted an enlarged navy; his method of governing required more and more funds; but his subjects were already so heavily taxed he dare not approach them.

Again it was Cromwell who came up with the answer: the monasteries. Cromwell, now in charge of just about every function of government and very well informed about the monasteries due to his earlier work under Cardinal Wolsey, filled Henry's mind with facts and figures about the wealth of these ecclesiastical establishments and the compelling need to abolish them. Further, he convinced Henry they were dangerous to the Crown and needed to be nationalized. The King consented and the results were astounding.

The King, with the aid of Cromwell, now his Vice Regent in all Ecclesiastical matters, had a great time disposing of some 578 monasteries; 130 convents; and dispossessing thousands of monks and nuns. Land and buildings were sold at bargain prices. In addition, gifts of some of the properties were made by a generous King to his favorites in the Court. Cromwell received six properties; his nephew, Richard received seven properties. In addition to the land, the precious metals that were confiscated from these properties amounted to a King's fortune. This would become the basis for the fortune of a later Cromwell who was destined to play a role in the fate of England and a place called Little Gidding.

Because the Knight Hospitalers of St. John held so many of these properties, including Little Gidding, and were thought to be a threat to the crown, the Order was disbanded, and the Grand Prior deposed. At least three English Knights were executed for refusing to take the oath of supremacy. Strangely enough, Henry granted William Weston, the deposed Grand Prior, a lifetime pension of 1,000 pounds a year. Sadly, though, William never lived to enjoy it. He died on the very day that the main Priory in London was destroyed. His effigy can be seen in the rebuilt church in Clerkenwell.

Somewhere along the line the arch manipulator, Thomas Cromwell, who was now roundly hated by most of the people of England, overstepped his authority and lost the support of his King. In what must be one of the great ironies of history in July, 1540, just months after the dissolution of the monasteries had been completed, Cromwell lost his head in the Tower of London. King Henry VIII, died a few years later in 1547 and was succeeded by his son, Edward, age 10.

An examination of the brass plaque in the church at Little Gidding reveals that King Edward was never listed as a Patron of the little church. One can speculate that this omission was caused by the fact that the lad was raised by his "Regent" to be a follower of Martin Luther, and a staunch Protestant. His father, King Henry VIII, for all he fought with the Papacy never considered himself a Protestant. In fact, at one stage Henry had so decried Luther's theses in his writings, the Pope had given him the title, "Defender of the Faith," a title which the crown uses to this day.

Whether Little Gidding was simply ignored during this period is unknown. No records exist to show what happened to it after the dissolution. For certain it did not disappear.

While I was pondering this conundrum, I heard a strange sound—a sort of humming—coming from the southwest Nave window above which was an inscription from the twenty sixth Psalm:

I LOVE THE HABITATION OF THINE HOUSE

Sitting on the bench beneath the inscription was an old lady! I gasped. Henry had two daughers, Mary and Elizabeth. But Elizabeth did not become Queen for many years after her father died. It had to be . . . !

"Yes it is I, Mary Tudor," she said, *"And I love this little church."*

To this I made no response. In fact, I was holding my breath. But the lady seemed not notice me as she went on speaking.

"That bastard Cromwell had the most to do with the closing of the monasteries but I saw to it that he did not harm this property which was neither sold nor given away. He lost his head in the end. And that was even before my brother took the throne."

Edward was her half brother, I thought to myself. But she went on without a pause.

"I've been watching you closely for some time,

young man, and you know that because I was a female, Edward, the son of Jane Seymour, robbed me of my rightful succession to the throne of England," she snorted loudly.

For the life of me I did not know what to make of her. She seemed to be humming a song and talking to me at the same time. Without lifting my head, I attempted to study her through the top of my glasses. Her hands appeared to be trembling and her head was shaking. Was that spittal at the corner of her mouth? I had read somewhere that Mary Tudor at the end of her life was so forlorn over her disappointment at not getting pregnant that she was virtually insane. In addition, when the plague of ague fever struck London she came down with it. That illness together with having suffered from dropsy most of her life had made the first Sovereign Queen of England a very sick "old" lady at the age of 42.

I became very uneasy at the thought I was in the presence of the ghost of Queen Mary and prepared to leave. But in a much more commanding voice, the lady stopped me.

"Do not leave, my good man, I have much I can tell you in your search for what happened at Little Gidding. You see it was I who restored this church as well as other preceptories and monasteries. Why, I even re-instated the Order of St. John which my father had dissolved. I made my friend, Sir Thomas Tresham, Grand Master, but I did not name him patron of the church. I retained the property for myself and my husband, Philip. Not bad for a crazy, sick 'old' lady, eh?"

"Look for yourself," she said as she pointed at the brass plaque. I looked and the entry read:

1554 - King Philip and Queen Mary, Patrons
She continued, *"I never had children. My menstrual*

periods were so irregular I feared I could never have a child. I was a virgin when I got married and again I was so irregular I made believe I was pregnant. That's why Philip left me and returned to Europe. But then I wasn't much good to him. He was a hot-blooded Spaniard and ten years younger than I. The real passion of my life was my church, the Roman Catholic Church."

"First, my father and then that juvenile, Edward, tried to keep me from my church. Why, Edward would not let me attend Mass so I had to do so in my chambers while he was on the throne which, thanks be to God, was less than five years. But it really wasn't all Edward's fault," she said, patronizingly.

"It was another Thomas, whose name was Cranmer and he was a doctor of divinity from Cambridge who manipulated Edward into being a Protestant. Henry had made Thomas Cranmer, Archbishop of Canterbury, when Thomas More refused to support him in his fight with the Pope. It was Cranmer who undertook to be Edward's tutor. So from his early childhood, the lad was taught terrible things about the Catholic Church and about His Holiness, the Pope."

Such as? I wondered.

"Such as," she mimicked, *"doing things the like of which had never been seen in a Christian country—eating meat openly during Lent; eliminating Latin from the Mass and substituting English. And then of all things, preparing not one but two new prayer books and having them approved by the Parliament and not the Pope. Of all things . . . ,"* she repeated almost to herself.

"I must say, though," she went on, *"in those new prayer books the Archbishop didn't stray very much from Catholic ritual even though he did omit the sacrificial character of the Mass. Before Edward died, Cranmer had the*

lad order the removal of all prayer books but his from every church. Anyone, who claimed the supremacy of the Pope or affirmed the Real Presence in the Eucharist, was a heretic. All of this he did in the name of King Edward, all of fifteen years old."

This last comment was made in a suddenly high pitched voice and I winced.

"Did you know, sir, did you know," she continued, *"that all this time most of the people remained Catholic and were scandalized when Edward was persuaded before he died to settle the crown on my second cousin, Lady Jane Seymour? I'll tell you a secret. He thought she was a Protestant but she really wasn't. But the idea that she would replace me on the throne came to naught. Not that they didn't try. When the Privy Council proclaimed her Queen why she fainted dead away. When she recovered, the Council again proclaimed her Queen. But when the soldiers were ordered to capture me they refused to obey and that was the end of that."*
"Shortly after, I was declared the legal Sovereign of England. Did my subjects ever rejoice! There was dancing in the streets. I was so happy. My twenty-two years of humiliation were over. Why, when I entered London, a city that had grown half Protestant because of the influx of Flemish immigrants, the entire populous, even those Protestants, came to greet me. Did you know, sir, did you know," she repeated herself, *"even my sister, Elizabeth, was at the gate, too?"*
"I was so happy. I was so happy," the first Sovereign Queen of England, kept crooning.

While she did so I had the opportunity to study her more closely. Then it struck me, she was not old at all! She was only a few years over forty but grief, illness and a tor-

tured life had taken an awful toll on what had been a frail
body. Her features were plain, almost masculine, but here
again the life she had been forced to live showed in the terrible wrinkles in her face and forehead. Her once reddish
hair was streaked with gray.

My mind wandered as I looked around the small
sanctuary. Why would a Queen, even such a piteous one as
Mary, restore this seemingly insignificant place? It made
no sense to me. Then I heard another voice—it had a for-
eign accent. Quickly I looked at Queen Mary but she was
looking at a figure seated next to her, shrouded in shadows.

"I can explain," a strong voice said without a quaver.

*"Two weeks before her nineteenth birthday, Mary
became desperately ill. My husband's second wife, Anne
Boleyn, was suspected of poisoning her. By this time I had
been banished to a Dulce's residence near Huntingdon.
When I heard of my daughter's illness and that no one appeared to be helping her, I begged Henry to let me nurse
her back to health. He agreed, but being Henry he did so in
his own strange, machiavellian way. Mary would be moved
to a place near me but I could not see her, only my apothecary could. Being Spanish, the apothecary had a wonderful
assortment of pills and draughts."*

*"In time, Mary recovered but we were still forbid-
den to see one another so we corresponded secretly. Then
Mary remembered this place. As you now know, when the
monasteries were closed, the crown retained a few of the
religious properties that were not worthy of selling. This
was one of them. Being so small and so remote, it had been
left alone and continued as a Catholic sanctuary as it had
been since it was built and, God willing, so will it always
remain."*

As she uttered the last words, I could see her hand
reach out and cover one of Mary's. It was then I regained

my wits and realized the voice belonged to Catherine of Aragon, Henry VIII's first wife, and in her mind and that of her daughter's, still his only wife.

The voice continued.

"History does not record it, but we heard Mass in this sanctuary several times, with only a Catholic priest present and, of course, a guard at the door. Few people even knew of our secret trysts. But then few people in England remember Mary. There is no monument to her anywhere in this country, even though she made a dying request for a decent memory of us."

I was saddened by her story and cast my eyes downward not looking at the apparitions of two of the most tragic women in English history. When I looked up, the ghost of Catherine of Aragon had disappeared but her daughter's ghost was still with me.

Mary now spoke in a much softer voice.

"I tried. I tried very hard. In the beginning of my reign, I visited the poor. I restored endowments to the universities, and did all sorts of good works. Why, I even pardoned those who had tried to keep me from the throne. I made them pay heavy fines so I could reduce taxes on the common folks. Within a few months of my coronation I declared that I would not compel or constrain consciences in the matter of religious belief. It was the first proclamation of religious tolerance by any government. But I was naïve. A few days after the proclamation, the chaplain of one of the bishops had a knife thrown at him from a crowd that resented his Catholic preaching. I was scared to death and very angry. I had tried to preach tolerance and it did not work."

She sounded like a woman scorned. Her voice now

became firm and strong.

> *"I sent a messenger to the Pope to allow full Catholic ritual restored to our churches. But the Pope on the advice of my soon to be father-in-law, Charles of Spain, refused saying the time was not ripe."*
>
> *"I appealed to Parliament to act but they went halfway. They told me I was no longer to be considered a bastard. Wasn't that nice of them? Then they repealed all of Edward's actions. But they flatly refused to restore any monasteries and other religious properties, except those belonging to the crown. And, of all things, they would not hear of any return of papal sovereignty over the church and instead made me the head of the English Church!"*
>
> *"Do you know why? Do you know why?"* the ghost was now shouting at me, and I was frightened into shaking my head from side to side.
>
> *"I'll tell you, then. There was hardly an influential family in England that did not hold property taken from the church. Oh, they were still a minority but they had the power of the purse and did they use it. There was no way they wanted the return of papal sovereignty over the Church. They feared the Pope would insist on a return of the monastic properties. And they secretly longed for and schemed to return Elizabeth to the throne. But I fooled them and found a lover at the same time."*

The quaver had left her voice; the lady sitting under the window seemed to straighten up on her bench and assume a more regal air. No longer was she the querulous 'old' lady. The atmosphere of the church now seemed charged with a tension I had not noticed before. I was apprehensive. Wasn't this Queen also known as "Bloody" Mary?

If she read my thoughts, she ignored them as she kept right on talking.

> *"My friend, Charles V, the ruler of Spain, thrilled*

*me with a new thought. He offered me his son, Philip, and
even pledged the Netherlands as a gift if we should produce
a male heir. The half-Spanish blood in me stirred at the
prospect of a political and religious union between England and Spain. Having been raised by a Spanish mother,
though, I was unaware of the depth of distrust the English
people felt for a foreigner on the throne, especially a Spaniard. All hell broke loose all over the land aided, I was certain, by those who held the former church properties and
feared they would be seized by the Roman church once a
Spanish prince was beside me on the throne of England."*

*"I tried to allay the concerns of my people by offer-
ing not to condemn the traitors who led the riots. But my
advisers, including my future father-in-law, were against it.
I must act, they said, or all would be lost. I guess I pan-
icked. To my sorrow, I ordered the conspirators executed.
However, when Charles wanted me to put Elizabeth to
death for her suspected role in conspiring against me, I refused."*

*"But it was not because of gibbeting the Protestants
I was called 'Bloody Mary.' The hatred between Catholics
and heretics, and Protestants and Catholics, had seen many
more people gibbeted than those I had executed."*

"No," she sighed, *"it was a hateful man who gave
me that awful title. His name was John Knox. A leader of
the Protestants who was safely ensconced in Geneva, and
full of hatred for all the women who held the throne in
countries he hoped would follow his teachings: Catherine
de Medici in France; Mary of Lorraine in Scotland; and
until recently Charles' sister, Mary, in Geneva and myself
in England."*

*"Knox maintained that Godfearing men everywhere
should denounce the plague of females before they utterly
destroyed God's church. He believed the Holy Bible itself
condemned a woman's right to be Queen, so he lashed out
at us in a tract, which, being a coward, he published anon-*

*ymously. It was entitled **FIRST BLAST OF THE TRUM-
PET AGAINST THE MONSTROUS REGIMENT OF
WOMEN.** In it he referred to me as a 'bloody tyrant'. I
made the mistake of having it banned by royal proclamation which, of course, only made people who never heard of
it want to read it. The label stuck and was followed by others that were so vicious they robbed me of whatever peace
of mind I had left. Forever after, I was referred to as
'Bloody Mary' and it was so unfair."*

The spirit of Mary Tudor paused and then she said,

*"Whenever you hear someone quietly praying in this
little sanctuary you will know I am here."*

This last sentence was said so softly I almost missed
it. And with that, the ghost of Queen Mary left me. I sat for
a long time, almost grieving for the 'old' lady, not knowing
what to make of her story but thankful that, quite possibly,
she had found some moments of solace in this small sanctuary tucked away in a forgotten corner of England.

Mary Tudor died in 1558 and Henry's other daughter, Elizabeth, ascended the throne of England with an offer
from the ubiquitous Philip to become his wife. This occurred in 1559, the year she became Queen. Elizabeth,
however, was a much sharper female than Mary; aware that
the Spanish King was scheming to obtain a dispensation
from the Pope's edict which forbade a man from marrying
his widow's sister, she very cleverly had one of her aides
inform him that she could not marry him because she was a
non-believer!"

I glanced at the brass plaque, there was no change
on it until 1590!

From my study of the period I knew this could not
be possible. Elizabeth was the Queen of England from 1559
to 1603. The plaque had to be incorrect—or so I thought.

Queen Mary had not mentioned any peculiarity as
to her patronage of the tiny church. I decided to turn my at-

tention to Philip. He had already played a significant role in the troubled history of England and had now made advances to Elizabeth.

What I discovered startled me. Even though Parliament flatly refused to name him King of England when he married Mary, the coronation record officially declares:

"Philip and Mary, by the grace of God, king and queen of England, France, Naples, Jerusalem and Ireland, Defenders of the Faith, Princes of Spain and Sicily, Archdukes of Austria, Dukes of Milan, Burgundy and Brabant, Counts of Hapsburg, Flanders and Tyrol."

It seems that Philip, in fact, believed he held a hereditary claim to the throne of England on his mother's side and not because he had married the English Queen. He could trace his descent to two forebears who had both married daughters of John of Gaunt, the son of Edward III.

But Philip had an even more compelling reason to covet the English throne. He was not satisfied that the empire over which he reigned outside of England was, geographically, the largest ever controlled by a monarch of that era: Spain, Portugal, Sicily, Naples and Milan, parts of the Netherlands and France; the Spanish and Portugese dominions in America, Africa and India.

In his mind his other title was of greater importance: "His Most Catholic Majesty."

Philip believed with all his heart that he was appointed by God to defend the Catholic church against all infidels and heretics. The Pope may be the Vicar of Christ on earth, but Philip considered himself God's champion on earth. And Elizabeth had turned him down by sassily declaring *"she could not marry him because she was a heretic!"*

Was the tiny church at Little Gidding involved in Philip's scheming? Or did Elizbeth just ignore it because she had greater things on her mind? I had now come to realize that nothing about this place was ever simple or uncomplicated—and that T. S. Eliot had come to the same conclusion!

Philip's ties with England had, in fact, been severed when Mary died and Elizabeth became Queen—but not so in his mind. For a long time he secretly believed that he would some day rightfully claim the throne of England. It did not deter him in the least, that twelve kings and queens of England who had reigned since Edward III were all descendants of the same line.

But to think of the Spanish King solely in respect to royal prerogatives is to ignore the inner force which really drove him: Catholicism. Queen Elizabeth, when she so haughtily snubbed him by telling him that she was a heretic, had rubbed salt into an already festering wound, and she would spend most of her reign regretting it. I wondered whether her failure to change the listing on the plaque in the church at Little Gidding and her disdain for even bothering with the place was another way of taunting him.

Once again this small, seemingly insignificant church seemed to be at the crossroads of the great conflicts surrounding it. Would it ever be so? No wonder Eliot used such strange metaphors to try to explain the history of this place:

> See, now they vanish, the faces and places . . .to
> become renewed, transfigured in another pat-
> tern.

I wondered whether the ghost of Elizabeth would appear and talk about the situation in England when even the bishops refused to officiate at her coronation. Probably not. Although she would go down in history as one of England's greatest monarchs, she would also be known for having a passion to postpone things—just put them off until the last minute. Would that "passion" explain why thirty-six years would elapse before she had her name listed on the brass plaque?

I left that speculation aside to imagine what fun it

would be to meet—even as a ghost—the tall, bright-eyed, intelligent redhead who ruled England for the rest of the sixteenth century and who was so beloved by her countrymen.

Before dealing with "Good Queen Bess," as she came to be known, it would be well to consider the moral landscape which she inherited after fifty years of turbulent, bloody religious ferment—a ferment which unfortunately would not end with her reign or those to follow. As indicated, she arrived on the scene years after the monasteries had been destroyed. The religious life of the monks and the nuns had been seriously impugned, and the religious houses were now mostly owned or leased by an entirely new group of people: the landed gentry. Although the majority of Englishmen considered themselves Catholics, the removal of the authority of the Pope had seriously undermined the concept of the intercessory role of the medieval Church.

Into this atmosphere of change came still another factor: the younger generation. Located mainly in London and inspired by followers of John Calvin they were bedazzled by a new concept of religion. One that used only the Holy Bible, in English, as guide for their faith and practice, and placed the Christian in direct communion with God. A concept that made unnecessary the worship of saints and relics, and even questioned the necessity of an episcopacy!

But overriding this new concept was a Pope who was still to be reckoned with and King Philip of Spain, the self-appointed Champion of God—whose name was still on the brass plaque.

It would be the height of foolishness to maintain that the preceding few paragraphs would explain the debate about the relationship of man with God that was carried on with great learning, savage intensity and brutal intolerance for not only the life of Queen Elizabeth but for centuries to come. They may serve, however, to explain what a brilliant woman she was to have handled the most complex religious and political situation of her time, and still remain beloved by her people and by history. But we get ahead of our story.

The more specific dimensions of this moral landscape are best described by the series of events which occurred at the moment the Parliament was informed that
Queen Mary had died and had been succeeded by Elizabeth. Nicholas Heath, Lord Chancellor and Archbishop of
York, in making the announcement praised Queen Mary's
devotion to the Catholic Church, but said not a word about
Elizabeth's.

In fact, the new Queen followed the beliefs of her
mother, Anne Boleyn, who was a Protestant: actually Anne
was a follower of Luther and probably called a Lutheran as
the word Protestant did not come into use until years later.
Further, the precedent established by Elizabeth's father,
King Henry VIII, made her the Supreme Head of the
Church of England. But as so often happens in history,
once a leader comes into power he or she does not always
follow the expectations of their supporters or detractors.
Such would prove to be the case when Elizabeth began her
rule.

She faced a Privy Council (still composed of Mary's
most intimate advisers) which was Catholic, as were the
bishops, the justices of the peace and most of the English
people. Further, Elizabeth was aware that her country was
still upset over the loss of Calais—an area along the coast
of Europe which England had ruled for over three hundred
years, and which had been lost by some misguided actions
of Queen Mary. So the idea of imposing a heretical religion
on England at that moment was thought to be out of the
question. Yet, Elizbeth knew that the activists of the younger generation, mostly in London and the south, were ex-
pecting her to take action that would follow their new beliefs in the doctrine of justification by faith alone without
the trappings of the medieval church of Rome.

At twenty-six, Elizabeth was a strong-minded woman: emotionally, religiously, and in likes and dislikes. On
one hand, she loved the crucifix and the splendid vestments
of the clergy: all of which were loved by the Catholics and
hated by the Protestants. On the other hand, she disliked the
Mass and its central theme that Christ was bodily present in

the Communion bread and wine, known theologically as the Real Presence and the most fundamental issue to Catholics next to acceptance of the authority of the Pope. In fact, almost every martyr who had been sent to the stake had been accused of the heresy of not believing in the Real Presence.

But Elizabeth was also a master politician. Any religious changes would be introduced in an orderly, lawful way under her authority. There were to be no riots, no destruction of churches, no attacks on Catholic preachers. The Papal Legate's secretary in England was so enthralled by her actions, he immediately informed the Vatican that Elizabeth would uphold the Catholic religion in England!

But the bishops surmised differently. When Heath, the Archbishop of York, had refused to crown her Queen he set an example for other bishops to follow his lead. Finally, Owen Ogelthorpe, the bishop of Carlisle, agreed to perform the ceremony, arguing that if no Catholic placed the crown on her head she would be embraced by the heretics. However, she was crowned as she, and not the bishops, planned! On Sunday, January 15, 1559, Elizabeth was crowned, Queen of England, in Westminster Abbey. After Oglethorpe had crowned her, a Mass was held in Latin, but the celebrant, Elizabeth's chaplain, spoke the words of consecration in English and did not elevate the host. The die was cast for a never-ending feud between the Crown and the Roman Catholic Church.

Many historians assert that Elizabeth helped move England from a medieval nation to a more progressive, modern one. The more one studies her, the more one is inclined to recognize that she was England's and the world's first modern woman. On the shameful side, is the revelation that she was abused as a fifteen year-old teen-ager by Lord Admiral Seymour, the husband of her stepmother, Catherine Parr. On the positive side, are her reactions as a woman to the leadership role of a nation. Before her first Parliament she carefully changed the Privy Council to one that was balanced between those from Mary's reign and those who held other beliefs. This was but her first demonstration that, as a woman, she could handle more ambiguity and uncertainty than most men. In fact, when John Knox tried to make up to her, she shrugged off his wish to visit her at court. She informed him, that although she might be considered by him to be inferior to a man as ruler she was not so considered by God, else why would He ordain her to be Queen! Knox never got the point.

In a further step before her first Parliament met, she adroitly refused to give the Crown's customary preferences to the mayors in the boroughs and the sheriffs in the counties as to whom should be chosen Ministers of Parliament from their districts. She left the choice up to the local people. She knew the House of Lords was made up primarily of Bishops and that the make-up of the House of Commons which would result from these local elections would give a clearer indication of the feelings of the people about the religious controversy. Her intuition as a woman paid off. A majority of Ministers elected supported an alteration in the prevailing religious practices. She then completely befuddled this group of men with her opening statement by telling them she would never marry, and in the end she told them,

> *"(it) shall suffice for me . . . that a marble stone shall declare that a Queen having reigned such a time, lived and died a virgin . . . "*

With that bit of dissimulation to chew on, the Parliament turned to the question of religion. When they proposed that Elizabeth would be known as the "Supreme Head of the Church," she demurred and proposed she be called the "Supreme Governor of the Church." She also proposed that the penalty for refusing to take the Oath of Supremacy, be, not death, but a fine or loss of office.

On March 18, 1559, two months and a day after her coronation, the Parliament restored the royal supremacy over the Church of England with only the Bishops and two others objecting. The next day, Palm Sunday, Elizabeth following one of Luther's early ideas decreed that communion in every church be administered in the two forms of bread and wine. However, she added an idea of her own: if any parish priest refused to administer the bread and wine to the congregation separately as the Protestants preferred, the people were to go to another church.

The matter of the marriage of priests, another of Luther's ideas, which was as unpopular with Elizabeth as it was with many of her subjects, was dealt with just as tactfully: that section of the Act of Mary's Parliament prohibiting it was repealed without making any mention as to what the section contained—an adroit legal manuever. Soon thereafter, Parliament approved the Act of Uniformity, as it was called, which introduced the Third Book of Common Prayer, abolished the Catholic Mass and restored the Protestant communion service.

In addition to religious matters, the young Queen was faced with very practical ones. Trade and money were as important to the survival of sixteenth century England as they are to any modern nation today. The young Queen was aware of and fascinated by both. Philip's occupation of the Netherlands and the seeming unending religious wars in France made the return of Calais impossible to achieve, but instead produced an unexpected dividend for England, one that Philip would live to regret.

Many of the refugees now fleeing the strife on the continent were highly skilled craftsmen. Elizabeth with her keen intuitive sense ordered these people be given every aid, regardless of religious belief. Her humane policy produced untold dividends. The manufacture of parchment and paper, steel instruments, felt, silk-weaving, thread, lace and glass, among others, became profitable industries. Antwerp, a city in the Netherlands, had been the financial exchange center but the wars had virtually shut it down. With the aid of an astute English financier, Thomas Gresham, Elizabeth opened a Royal Exchange of England in London. Thus, in a remarkably short time, England, a tiny isolated and quite backward island nation, began its inexorable march to greatness. Further, the astute young Queen began investing some of this new wealth in building ships, something her father had started before he ran out of money.

But as every coin must have two sides, so every fortune usually has a misfortune. Elizabeth's astuteness in aiding the refugees for commercial reasons brought her much grief on matters of religion. Among the flood of immigrants were those who had fled England during the latter days of Queen Mary. Most of these had lived in Geneva and had become followers of John Calvin and were bent on bringing the "new" religion to England in such a way as to purify the new Church of England of what they considered to be the unscriptural, Catholic forms of worship. Quickly named "Puritans," they divided along two entirely different models for substituting Calvinistic models of ecclesiastical polity and liturgy.

Some were moderate Puritans who along with some Bishops felt that while Scripture was the perfect model of faith, on matters of discipline and church government these should be left to the civil magistrate—the Crown and Parliament. Other more radical Puritans maintained that on matters of discipline as well as doctrine and structure nothing should be imposed that could not be proven in Scripture.

It would have been difficult enough if Elizabeth had been caught between those two opposing camps, but other groups of refugees brought her even more grief. Some from the Netherlands included Dutch Anabaptists who held the "civil magistrate" in complete contempt. (Some of these would later be put to death, some would be deported.) Others were followers of a Dutch theologian by the name of Arminius, who rejected Luther's thesis of salvation by faith, and taught that it was man's good works that brought salvation. (The followers of Arminius would later be considered disguised Catholics as we shall soon discover.)

From France came still others to bedevil the Queen. The Pope had established at Douai, France, a seminary led by a man named, William Allen, an English Catholic. It was Allen's mission to train Jesuits to infiltrate England and secretly to evangelize Englishmen who thought of leaving the Catholic Church and thereby, over time, bring the now so-called Church of England back under the Holy See in Rome.

And so, all the while Elizabeth believed she was adroitly handling the church-state issue, and leading her nation on new paths in commerce and finance, her humane decision to admit immigrants from the continent steadily produced new and more dangerous problems for her reign. Problems that would plague her the rest of her life.

As I pondered still another conundrum, I happened to look over at the brass plaque. A small figure now sat beneath it.

Elizabeth!

"No," a voice said with asperity, *"her Mother."*

I was stunned. Could it be Anne Boleyn? She was known to have a fiery temper and was extremely wily. If so, I had better watch my step with her ghost. I should not have worried as she had paid me scant attention, and just continued talking.

" . . . also you have been most accurate in your description about my daughter's life. But there are many things you do not know—that only a mother could know."

I was about to speak but thought better of it.

"It is said that she never uttered my name in her entire life. Be that as it may, I was never far from her in spirit and she knew that. She even closed her eyes when she ordered the execution of Mary of Scotland, and thought of me. She knew I believed in the occult, too."

I now wondered why the ghost of Anne Boleyn would interrupt my train of thought about immigrants to tell me this story.

"Give me time, give me time. I'll get to that. I'll get

to that."

So she could read my thoughts!

"I wanted you to know how close I was to Elizabeth even though I lost my head when she was only a baby, two years old. Only a mother, even a dead one, can know when her child is going through an awful travail, and that is what she suffered with those who were not satisfied with her patience in dealing with the religious questions."

"She tolerated those Jesuits for a long time. But then came Philip's Armada. He had tried every device to bring England back into the Roman Catholic Church; he even tried to have my daughter assassinated. Nothing worked. Then he decided to invade England with the largest fleet of ships ever assembled. But they were repulsed by our ships, especially the fireships, and also by the fury of the weather in the Channel and the North Sea. England was saved."

What, I wondered, did this have to do with the Jesuits?

"I'm getting to that if you will just give me time," she answered with annoyance in her voice.

"It was in 1590, just two years after the defeat of the Armada, that Elizabeth became completely fed up. Why? When William Allen, who had left Douai to be made a Cardinal in Rome, called her 'an incestuous bastard, begotten in sin and born of an infamous courtesan . . .who hath abused her body . . . by unspeakable and incredible variety of lust,' and demanded that the Catholics of England should rise against this 'depraved, accursed, excommunicate heretic,' she lost her patience. This led her to do things her nature rebelled against. She persecuted the Jesuits the same way the Roman Church had persecuted heretics during the

Inquisition. Now look here at this plaque."

I did as I was told.
It read:

1590 - Queen Elizabeth, Patron

"You will notice," she continued, "it shows the year Elizabeth declared herself Patron of this church. It was at this time that all Roman Catholic churches became part of the Church of England. Elizabeth had tried not to be dogmatic; she had tried to subdue her emotional convictions but the Jesuits would not be silenced so she had to deal firmly with them and she did."

"For years my poor Elizabeth was beset on all sides by religious tempests, so to speak. Not so much an organized system as a kind of force that could assume different dimensions. Some wanted simply to make some changes in the Church of England; others wanted to separate from the Church and start their own churches, and of all things even name their own ministers of the gospel. They wanted to do away with Bishops, vestments, sacred images, even the cross!"

Her voice trailed off and I wondered what she was about to reveal about this place but to my surprise she did not continue talking about the church but went on to an entirely different subject. One that really bewildered me.

"You see, as I said earlier, there is much I can tell you that you may not find in any book. Elizabeth is known as the greatest Queen England ever had. She did much for her country and her people but only her Mother can know how much she suffered and what kind of help she sought when she was bewildered. It is known of course that Elizabeth consulted Doctor Dee, an astrologer, as to the date of

her coronation, the most important date in her life. But no one knows better than I how many other times she consulted Doctor Dee and other astrologers. You see she was my daughter every bit as much as Henry's and many people called me a witch who bewitched Henry into marrying me."

"When I was a young girl at the nunnery in Hever, one of the nuns claimed to foretell the future, and to be in direct touch with God through Mary Magdalene. I believed her. Also, I have two body marks that people claimed were associated with witchcraft: the large mole on my neck, and the extra little finger on my right hand—just a teeny extra nail. And of course, my wonderful dog, a wolfhound named Urian. You do know that name, don't you?"

I was so startled I shook my head vigorously.

"It is one of the names used by Satan!"

Why was she telling me all these things?

"I'll tell you why," she said acidly, *"because it is important to your study. England during my days and the days of my daughter was not the England you know. Like all rulers of governments of her time, Elizabeth believed that some religion, or some supernatural source, was necessary to the social order and the stability of the state. In the conflicts between the different beliefs that were being espoused by the leaders and thinkers of the Church, she found only confusion, hostility and hatred—and in the end torture and death. What was she to do as a lonely woman and a Queen? So you see, she found it necessary to turn to the occult for personal help. It was not the first time the head of state would do so. And it would not be the last, you should know that."*

Yes, I thought to myself, now that I think about it,

she's right.

She paused and I thought she was about to vanish. But not Anne Boleyn. She continued talking.

"Something else you may not have thought about," *she continued, "is the absence of any reference to religious* *conflict in any of the literature or drama produced during* *Elizabeth's reign, and there was much of it. But William* *Shakespeare in his play, 'Love's Labor Lost,' refers to the* *occult:*

> "'O paradox! black is the badge of hell,
> the hue of dungeons and the school of night.'"

Where, I wondered, was she taking me with this line of thought.

"That is the end of it," she said almost angrily. *"I* *wanted you to have some appreciation for Elizabeth's turn-* *ing to seers when she was beset on every side by religion-* *ists who bedeviled her with conflicting views of Christ's* *Church."*

She paused and I looked above her head at the brass plaque. The next entry startled me. It read:

1591 - Revoked

This time the word was not "cessation," it was "re-voked!" Elizabeth must have changed her mind once again.

"She did," her mother said. *"Elizabeth made several* *attempts to thwart the efforts of the Jesuits. Finally, she de-* *cided to dissolve all the religious houses that had been re-* *founded by Mary Tudor: Little Gidding was among them."*

It had taken Elizabeth thirty-six years to make up

her mind to be the Patron of this tiny church and to abandon it a year later. When I looked down to ask the ghost of Anne Boleyn what had happened to the church, she was no longer there. I was still left with only part of the story. I became more than ever determined to pursue the story of this church.

3

THREE MEN ON A SCAFFOLD

Literary scholars for years have attempted to decipher Eliot's obtuse phrase, "Of three men, and more, on the scaffold. And a few who died forgotten. . . ." In my study of Little Gidding, increasingly I came to believe he was referring to the three men whose lives became folded into the tragic fate of this community so I decided to follow that path of reasoning. This is what I unearthed.

Queen Elizabeth never married and died childless. In the last years of her life, though, three male children were born who would have a profound impact in changing what some historians feel was her greatest achievement: to keep her nation at peace internally even though beset by mortal enemies abroad.

Even stranger is that the careers of these three men, in divers ways, would intersect at Little Gidding. Their life stories represent in microcosm the changes in England that had been brought about by the actions first of Elizabeth's father, King Henry VIII, and later by Queen Elizabeth herself. As before mentioned, in selling off the monasteries Henry unwittingly created in England a new class of untitled nobility known as the "landed gentry." This was a social group situated between the nobility and the freeholders who owned a farm or small tract of land. The King had profited handsomely from the sale of these monastic properties but there were some he gave as gifts to intimates and admirers while other properties remained in the control of the royal family.

For her part, Elizabeth's magnanimity in encouraging immigrants from the continent to settle in London created a new "bourgeoise"—bankers, craftsmen, merchants, lawyers, manufacturers, physicians. This group, together with the "landed gentry," soon became hungry to share in the power of the nation, and found in the Parliament a vehicle to achieve this objective. Added to this revolutionary change in the social, economic and political order of England was the ongoing religious rivalry which would finally lead to the very disaster she sought so valiantly to avoid: Civil War. So it was into this caldron over a span of several years that these three men were born.

The first was Nicholas Ferrar who was born in London on February 22, 1593, three years after Elizabeth decided to become the Patron of the church at Little Gidding. He was born into the family of a wealthy London merchant who owned a large house in the city and another in the country. Nicholas's father was a merchant of such stature that Queen Elizabeth granted him the right to wear his family coat of arms with a new crest—undoubtedly a high privilege since it was later worn by all his descendants. Nicholas Ferrar, the elder, was the head of the Skinner Company, a company that had extensive trade with the East and West Indies and other areas of commerce. Further, he was a great friend of Sir Walter Raleigh, Sir Francis Drake and other adventurous sailors who had explored the New World. He maintained a keen interest in the Virginia Company of London, a commercial trading company chartered by Elizabeth's successor, King James I, with the objective of colonizing the eastern American shore. An ardent member of the Church of England, he was supportive of the King and the State, doing whatever was required of him in this regard. Throughout his life, he maintained a keen interest in establishing Christianity in the colonies. His wife, Mary, who came from an ancient Cheshire family, was noted for her personal charm, character, keen intelligence and deep religious convictions. Mary was known by her friends to be a most pious woman.

The Ferrar's named their third child, Nicholas, Jr. At least four more children followed Nicholas, although the exact number seems to be a matter of some conjecture among the biographers of the Ferrar family. From all reports, Nicholas was a beautiful child with a fair complexion and light-colored hair like his mother but yet very delicate and given to frequent bouts of fever. It was evident from the start that he was a very bright child with an uncommon memory and a studious disposition. Scholars of the period have noted that by the age of five he could read perfectly every chapter of the Bible.

When he was eight years old he was entered into a school at Enborne, near Newbury, where his two older brothers, John and Erasmus, were students. About this time a rather mysterious thing happened to him which is worthy of note. It appears that he had difficulty sleeping and one night a fit of skepticism entered his mind (probably because since his very early years he was caused to read a chapter from John Foxe's *BOOK OF MARTYRS* every night). He began to doubt whether there was a God and, if there was, what was the best way to serve Him. At midnight of a cold and frosty night he rose, went down to the garden and stood for a long time thinking seriously of his doubt. He threw himself on the cold ground and cried aloud, "Yes, there is, there must be a God: and He, no question, if I will earnesly seek it of Him, will teach me not only how to know, but how to serve Him acceptably. He will be with me all my life here, and at the end hereafter will make me happy." This experience made an indelible impression on the lad's life and is reflected in the decision he made to change careers in the middle of an active business life.

At the age of thirteen, Nicholas entered Cambridge University where he took a Bachelor's degree at age seventeen and a Master's degree at age twenty. Throughout his brilliant progress in school, however, he was constantly beset with ill-health, probably aggravated by the dampness of the 'malarial fens' on which the city of Cambridge and the surrounding areas are built.

A few years before Nicholas entered Cambridge the second of the three men was born. His name was Oliver

Cromwell and he was born in Huntingdon on April 25, 1599, to Robert and Elizabeth Cromwell. Four days later he was baptized in the Church of St. John in Huntingdon. Oliver's father was the owner of property which had been given him by his father, Sir Henry Cromwell, one of the richest men in the district and known as the "Golden Knight." Sir Henry's property was part of the monastic lands obtained years before by Thomas and Richard Cromwell from a grateful King, Henry VIII.

Oliver's parents were part of the "landed gentry" who along with the Ferrars of London now moved to stage center in the dramatic developments which were about to descend upon "Merrie England" with the death of Queen Elizabeth.

In 1603, the year the Queen died, young Oliver entered a Free School attached to the Hospital of St. John in Huntingdon. The headmaster of the school, Dr. Thomas Beard, was known as a fierce Puritan who was anti-papist to the extent that he considered the Pope to be an Anti-Christ. Dr. Beard was a Cambridge graduate and a clergyman who was a stern but apparently empathic teacher who instilled great loyalty in his students.

In addition to the usual secular and religious studies offered at grammar schools of that time, Dr. Beard had his young charges study a work entitled *THE THEATRE OF GOD'S JUDGEMENTS* —an enormous collection of punishments, or providences as they were then called, which God would inflict upon transgressors. In short, the good doctor sought to impress his charges with the fear of a God who did not overlook nor forgive any shortcomings of those who believed in Him.

As we shall discover, this religious experience would have an impact on Oliver's later career. But for now it is necessary only to trace his progress as a young man. Physically, he was short and well-built but never fat. Mentally quite average but emotionally given over to bouts of melancholia—a factor that would show up later in life.

As Nicholas Ferrar before him, though not at such a

young age as Nicholas, Oliver entered Cambridge and apparently undertook the normal studies for a young man of his era since in later years he appears to have had a good command of Latin. But he was unable to complete his studies at Cambridge due to the sudden death of his father. Thus, at age eighteen he found himself the man of the house, so to speak, with the responsibility for his mother, several unmarried sisters and a small estate.

Some scholars believe he went to London and studied law at the Inns of the Court in the fashion of his grandfather and two of his uncles. While the records are unclear on that point, it is a well-documented fact that he met his future bride, Elizabeth Bourchier, the daughter of a London merchant, about the time he is reputed to have been a student in that city.

In addition to having studied at Cambridge as did Nicholas Ferrar, Oliver Cromwell also had strange religious experiences. At one point he fantasized about a large cross standing in the center of the town of Huntingdon. Later, he suffered from bouts of melancholia which seemed to be lessened only by his intense religious faith. Still later, he came to believe that he was a chosen instrument of God!

* * * * *

The third of the three men was born in Scotland, November 19, 1600. Also, a third child, the boy's name was Charles. His father was King James, VI, of Scotland; his mother, Anne, was the sister of the King of Denmark. Like Nicholas Ferrar, Charles was a sickly child. Indeed, he was so frail he was unable to travel to England with his parents when Queen Elizabeth died in 1603, and his father ascended the throne of England as King James I. In time, the young lad was brought to London where he joined his brother named Henry, and a sister named Elizabeth.

Short in stature all his life, he developed a stammer which apparently caused him to be withdrawn and shy around strangers. This condition was undoubtedly worsened by the death of his brother, Henry, in 1613, whom he loved dearly. A year later, he suffered a severe bout of loneliness when his sister, Elizabeth, left England to marry Frederick V, Count of the Palatinate (an area of the lower Rhine).

As with Nicholas and Oliver, Charles early in life developed deep religious feelings and, due to his father's teaching, he developed an intense belief in the "Divine Right of Kings." This belief held that Kings were intended by God to rule over man—a belief that would one day cause Charles and the people of England much pain and suffering.

Thus, it was in strange and mysterious ways that the lives of these three men—Nicholas Ferrar, Oliver Cromwell, and Charles—would become intertwined in the fate of the tiny church at Little Gidding in the most climatic period of English history.

*   *   *   *   *

Nicholas Ferrar's involvement with the family of Charles began because of his ill health. The longer he stayed at Cambridge the more his health failed. In the medical opinion of the time doctors felt his condition was due to the extreme dampness of the fen country in which the city was located. They urged upon the young man a very modern cure: travel. Nicholas had little choice but to agree. The Master of his hall (college), being a friend of the Royal Court, took Nicholas to meet Princess Elizabeth, Charles's sister, who being newly married to Count Frederick was planning an early departure for the continent. She was delighted to have the young man accompany her.

It was during this extensive trip that Nicholas displayed three interests that would have a direct bearing on his later life. One was his fascination for the economic aspects of each country he visited: industries, businesses, manufacturing and the like. A second was a curiosity about continental Protestantism, especially in the Netherlands. In that country, too, he exhibited a third interest: helping the poor.

The Protestants whom Nicholas visited were mainly those who had fled England because of the religious ferment that had threatened their lives and for which they had been thrown in jail. These included the Brownists or Separatists named after their founder, Robert Brown: small congregations who with their ministers felt they had the right as Christians to organize themselves for worship; formulate their own creed on the basis of scripture; choose their own church leaders, and live under no rule but that of the Holy Bible, and under no authority but Christ's. When Nicholas visited them they lived in Amsterdam but later they moved to the city of Leyden. In 1620, they left Leyden to begin their fateful voyage, via England, across the Atlantic Ocean in a small ship to the New World.

In time, Nicholas tired of the routine incumbent upon a person who traveled with a Princess and her Court, and decided to strike out on his own. Princess Elizabeth despaired of his leaving and urged him to become her Secretary at the Royal Court in Heidelberg, but Nicholas demurred and left with her blessing and Godspeed. He traveled extensively throughout Europe, at times with a companion but much of the time alone. Traveling alone, though, was hazardous for any young man; for Nicholas it was dangerous in the extreme. He was a frail young man subject to repeated bouts of ill health. In Europe, disease and disaster lurked around every corner. A journal he kept on the trip indicates that he fell ill several times and had to stay at length either with friends of his father or personal acquaintances from his days at Cambridge.

The journal also shows he escaped assassination on more than one occasion when he stayed at wayside inns. His greatest danger, however, appeared to come from the Jesuits. He came to feel that the Jesuits had prior knowledge of his visits with the English Protestants, and believed he had some ulterior motive in visiting around Europe. Then, too, his close connection with Princess Elizabeth whose father, King James, was a doctrinal Presbyterian when he was King of Scotland, no doubt caused the Jesuits to believe him dangerous to their cause.

It is of more than passing interest to record that even in those distant times it was the efficiency of the British Secret Service that warned him about the Jesuits. His visit to Rome was so closely followed by the Jesuits that Nicholas was cautioned to keep his intentions private, change his address daily, and even to wear different disguises!

It seems that most of Nicholas Ferrar's travels throughout Europe were filled with excitement and adventure but two episodes in particular seem to have a direct bearing on our story about Little Gidding. The first deals with his visit to the island of Malta where a Knight of the Order of St. John (by then known as the Knights of Malta) formed a particular friendship for Nicholas, and when he left made a gift to him of a bejeweled, eight-pointed cross. The second occurred during his visit to Marseilles where he was struck down with a life-threatening fever—the worst he had ever experienced. A kindly landlady gave him every possible care; her husband, catching sight one day of the dazzling Maltese cross, assumed he was a Knight traveling incognito!

In Spain he kept his movements obscure thinking perhaps he was in some danger from the Inquistion. Within a short time he received word of distress at home and a plea to return as soon as possible to help extricate the family from ruin. Nicholas now pursued a dangerous course of action: with little money he decided to travel on foot overland to San Sebastion on the coast and take a ship home. It appears that the remainder of his travels were beset with much risk to his life, and finally upon landing at Dover he fell flat on his face and offered his thanks to God for bringing him home safe and sound to his native country after such perilous times abroad.

While Nicholas Ferrar was being educated in the ways of the world at home and through perils abroad, not much is known of the hamlet and church at Little Gidding. Only two facts about the place and the area appear to have a bearing on future developments. One is that Charles's father, King James I, became Patron of the church in 1614;

the other that Nicholas's sister, Susanna, who had married
John Collett when Nicholas was seven years old, was now
raising a family at Bourne Bridge, a small town west of
Cambridge and at the beginning of the low hills above the
malarial fens, not too many miles from Little Gidding.

Nicholas visited his sister often after his return to
his parents home in London. He was offered a teaching ap-
pointment at Cambridge but refused it. Whether this was
due to the climate of that region or to the difficulties he
found in one of his father's business enterprises, which was
probably the reason for the distress call he received from
home, we do not know. What is known, though, is that for
the next five years of his life Nicholas led an amazingly
successful career. Because of it's bearing upon his future
life at Little Gidding, it deserves some considerable mention.

Charles's father not only authorized the publication
in 1611 of a revision of the Holy Bible, known forever after
as the King James Edition or Authorized Version, he also
chartered the London Company of Virginia, as mentioned
earlier. A few words of backgound of this endeavor are
necessary at this juncture. The Company was granted the
right to colonize and develop the land in America between
present-day North Carolina and Maryland. Sir Walter Raleigh had attempted to colonize this territory in 1580, and
called it Virginia after the Virgin Queen of England. The
endeavor failed and the colonists were carried back to England by his friend, Sir Francis Drake. In 1582, a group of
150 people were sent and, although they landed and moved
inland from Chesapeake Bay, no one is quite sure of their
fate as they were never heard of again.

After the defeat of the Spanish Armada, English
seamen again began reconnoitering the American coast.
Within a few years a renewed effort at colonization was un-
dertaken by King James I. The Virginia Company now dis-
patched several ships carrying over 100 colonists to the
New World. This group again entered Chesapeake Bay but
this time landed on a peninsula and, to the delight of their
sovereign, named it Jamestown. Sadly, though, this group

met with almost unmitigated disaster, and by 1609 the King was forced to reorganize the entire enterprise and called on some of the most important business leaders in London to do so. Among them was Nicholas Ferrar, Sr.

It is not surprising, given the high regard King James had for Nicholas Ferrar, that he soon became one of the leading shareholders in this new enterprise. In fact, records show that many meetings of the governing body of the Company now met at the Ferrar's home. One of the Ferrar's collateral interests in the Company was to establish a college for Christian teaching in the new colony.

It was during the years his son was traveling in Europe that the colony and the Company began to run into increasing difficulty both in America and at home in England. It is strange to note—in light of earlier difficulties England had with Spain—that King James not only reestablished relations with that country, but at his Court had a Spanish Ambassador who greatly influenced his thinking. The Spaniards, who had been granted dominion over all of the New World by a Pope of Spanish descendant, Alexander VI, in 1493, now worried that the English company was beginning to make inroads into their kingdom in the Americas. Consequently, the Ambassador did everything within his power to persuade King James that the leaders of the Company were dangerous schemers. He further alarmed the King by suggesting the colonists were drafting a democratic constitution that could become a direct threat to the English Crown.

For his own reasons, King James listened carefully to the Spaniard. On one hand, he thoroughly disapproved of a "noisome weed" called tobacco that the colonists were growing and the Company was selling (and which not so coincidentally was a threat to Spanish control of the market since tobacco was grown elsewhere in the Americas). On the other hand, the King had plans for his son, Charles, to wed the Spanish Infanta, and bring England and Spain closer together in a political alliance. Shades of earlier times!

In addition to these issues, some of the other leaders of the Company were not as virtuous and efficient as the

Ferrars. They were, in fact, corrupt and careless in the extreme. So much so, that the Virginia Company fell into financial trouble.

It was into this cauldron that Nicholas returned to London and engaged in the family business. Within a short time his father retired and died the following year. So, at the age of twenty seven, after having been away from home for five years and not in very good health, Nicholas was plunged head over heels into the leadership of the Virginia Company. His older brother, John, who had been serving as the chief administrative officer of the company after the scoundrels had been removed, now turned the reins over to his younger brother.

Nicholas now proved to be not only a man of high learning but also an astute business man as well: possessed of great judgment and administrative ability. The King was so impressed with his skills he wanted him to join his inner circle of advisers and become Secretary to the Privy Council, a post which Nicholas refused because of his dedication to helping the Company survive. But even with his great ability he could not stem the tide. In a short space of time catastrophe after catastrophe struck the colony and the Company. Jamestown was wiped out by the Indians, and King James, fed up with the whole operation, ordered the house arrest of Nicholas and the Treasurer and former Treasurer of the Company.

Remarkably, when they were brought before a Court of Inquiry and refused legal counsel, Nicholas chose to handle their defense. His arguments were so brilliant people began to attend the trial in such numbers that the Court finally ordered the spectators limited to twelve people. But the Court, wanting to follow the King's wishes, ruled against the Company. Nicholas, fearing the books would be confiscated, and under house arrest, secretly made copies of all of the transations of his administration. A prodigious feat which later proved to be a sagacious one.

Surprisingly, it was about this time Nicholas and one hundred shareholders of the Company were elected to Parliament. Both Nicholas and his brother, John, believed that Parliament would act to vindicate Nicholas's management of the Company. Alas, this did not happen. The King intervened and forbade Parliament to interfere in the matter. The Company was dissolved and the London Company of Virginia ceased to exist, and the territory was made a Royal Colony in 1624. (Of note is that another company called the Plymouth Company of Virginia, led by shareholders from Plymouth, Bristol and Exeter, had also been formed in 1606 to colonize the coast of the Americas from present day New Jersey to Maine. It was later called the Council of New England.)

With the demise of the London Company of Virginia, Nicholas now turned his attention to salvaging the remains of his father's wealth. Of interest is that part of the legacy was a parcel of land on Somers Island—now Bermuda—to be used for the Christian education of children. In addition to working on his father's estate, Nicholas also undertook the task of overseeing his brother John's financial affairs which were in a similar state of confusion. In time Nicholas, discovering the family's finances, except for his mother's, were in bad shape, made a momentous decision affecting not only his own but his family's future.It would also involve the fate of Little Gidding.

*   *   *   *   *

In the years Nicholas Ferrar was engaged in these enterprises, the other two men whose lives would impact Little Gidding, King Charles I, and Oliver Cromwell, wereliving quiet lives oblivious to the religious and political calamities that were about to embroil them, their country and the tiny hamlet in the midlands.

Charles, now heir apparent to the throne since his brother Henry died, was living a reserved, almost sheltered life. He was despondent over scurrilous stories, circulated by his enemies, saying he had murdered his beloved brother so he could seize the Crown when his father, James I, died. Because of his speech impediment and frail physique, he seldom left the Royal compounds. Consequently, he was almost completely isolated from the people whom he was destined to serve as Monarch.

Recluse or not, he appears to have developed several passions: horses, hunting, the arts and religion. In point of fact, at one time early in life his passion for religion led his brother to nickname him, 'the Archbishop'.

To avoid traveling abroad, he brought the Flemish artists, Van Dyke and Rubens, to London, along with other artists from the continent. Over time he became a very discriminating collector and a generous patron of the arts. He was able to pursue his love for horses and hunting among the vast estates owned by the Crown. Charles's almost complete isolation from his people, coupled with his parentage and later his marriage, would cause his ruin. From his father he acquired the conception that kings are intended to rule absolutely without regard to Parliament or its laws. In fact, Charles's earliest letters show a marked distrust of the House of Commons which by the time he became King was entirely in the hands of the 'landed gentry' of the countryside and the 'bourgeoisie' of London.

By coincidence, just as Nicholas Ferrar was about to terminate his affairs in London, Charles was taken on a trip to Spain by the notorious Duke of Buckingham, King James I's favorite minister. Buckingham's intention was to find a wife for Charles. Instead, Charles met and fell in love with a French Princess he met enroute, and developed such an intense hatred for Spain he pressed his father to go to war against the Spaniards.

On March 27, 1625, King James I died, and Charles at the age of 25 became King Charles 1, and married his French love, Henrietta Maria, sister of the French King Louis XIII, and an ardent Roman Catholic.

While Charles was thus preparing his place in history, the third man, Oliver Cromwell, was living the life of a country squire in the midlands of England. After his marriage to Elizabeth Bourchier in London, Oliver moved to Huntingdon, tended his small estate, and sired six children. His lands were largely devoted to raising wheat, and his income was barely sufficient to provide for a growing family and still maintain a position of respect in the community. Even so, he managed to impress his neighbors sufficiently to become actively engaged in local politics—an activity that would lead, in 1628, to his election to Parliament from Huntingdon.

No sooner was he elected to Parliament than his strongly held belief, as a Puritan, that the individual Christian could establish direct contact with God through prayer, and that the principal duty of the clergy was to inspire the laity through their preaching, clashed with the views of King Charles. The King strongly advocated the High Church Party, which stressed the use of the Prayer Book, the value of ritual and complete support of Bishops. The dispute over religious views annoyed the King. When Parliament also refused his request for financial aid to underwrite the cost of the abortive war he was engaged in with Spain, Charles dissolved Parliament in 1629, barely a year after Oliver Crowmwell had taken his seat in the House of Commons.

Neither Charles nor Oliver were aware that their differing perceptions of religion and the status to which they were born harbored the seeds of a conflict that would pit one man against the other in a civil war that would convulse England; pit Englishmen against Englishmen; destroy the tiny Church at Little Gidding; and cause the founding of a great nation across the sea. At issue was nothing less than the rights of people to control their own destiny in this world and the next. Because of his isolation from the people, Charles seems to have been oblivious that feudalism had virtually evaporated as the economic system of England.

Most of the land was now owned by the gentry and not the barons. This new class of land owners, along with merchants, professionals and businessmen in London, wanted political power commensurate with their economic status. Nor does he seem to have been aware that at the core of the religious controversy was a revolutionary idea: if people could decide for themselves God's will as stated in the Holy Bible, then they could apply the same principle to the control of their earthly destiny and not by the will of their King.

In his fecklessness, Charles thus brought about a union of religious and political discontent that would change the world. Oliver Cromwell, now tucked away in nearby Huntingdon and later, the town of Ely, may have had some inkling of future events since he had no less than nine cousins in Parliament. Also, as time went on, he grew even more strongly Puritan and became more active in local politics.

Meanwhile, Nicholas Ferrar, now out of the limelight and winding up his family's affairs in London, may have been more aware of the underlying currents sweeping across England than most of his contemporaries. Or, perhaps, he was more clairvoyant than anyone realized. It is true that many men and women, in centuries past and even in our time, have abandoned promising careers for a life in a monastery or in the church. Most have done so with the explanation that they felt a "call" to live a more religious life. Seldom has anyone done so without the slightest indication of the reason for their action. Nicholas Ferrar was the exception.

He gave up a career which every one of his biographers agree was at its zenith. Although he fought the Crown, the King wanted his service; he was offered ambassadorships; high positions in important companies; service in Parliament; professorships at Cambridge. The world was at his doorstep but he decided to retire from it to dedicate the rest of his life to God. As indicated, others have done so but have given explanations. Nicholas did not. The majority of his written words are still kept in the library at Cambridge University. His carefully written minutes of the Virginia Company are in the Library of Congress. But all of these records are silent on the most important decision of his life.

His decision was so unusual for a man of his talents it is tantalizing to speculate on the reason or reasons for it. There were several events in his life which could have a bearing on his decision. The first happened on his five year sojourn in Europe. It seems that while he was in Spain he had another of his strange visions: this time falling into a trance and hearing a voice urging him to go home at once, his family desperately needed him. He would later mention this episode, even repeating it on his deathbed.

The second is less ethereal. While in Parliament, he was called upon to aid in the prosecution of the Earl of Middlesex, one of the conspirators who ruined the Virginia Company. His brilliant speech was credited with the Earl's condemnation and execution. In a man as sensitive as Nicholas Ferrar, it is quite possible that instead of considering his performance a victory, he considered it a sin. The third, of course, could have been his health. Throughout most of his life he appears to have been seriously ill from time to time. The records of his trip to Europe are replete with stories of his bouts of serious illnesses. These appear to have diminished or been unreported during his epoch struggle to save the Virginia Company. But he appears never to have been completely well. It could be that he harbored premonitions of an early death. Finally, he appears to have been not only deeply religious but, as before mentioned, possessed of a great curiosity about the differing forms of religious beliefs that were emerging in the Christian church. There is no record of his activities in London in this regard but his five years on the continent were filled with visits and conversations with the leaders of the different sects in the countries he visited.

In 1626, at the age of 33, a short time after the demise of the Virginia Company and his brief tenure in Parliament, and borrowing from his Mother, he purchased property not many miles from where sister, Susanna, lived. It was located on the high ground beyond the fens between Huntingdonshire and Northamptonshire. It was a place called Little Gidding.

Having rejected marriage and declaring a life of celibacy, it was here Nicholas decided to spend the rest of his days. Whether he knew of the history of the tiny church and the property we do not know. And we can only speculate as to the reason he had to ask his mother for the money to purchase the property. In all probability, both Nicholas and his brother, John, had been unable to salvage the family fortune from the financial collapse of the Virginia Company. Consequently, it was necessary for his mother to use her resources to buy the property.

Surprisingly, the entire family decided to join him at Little Gidding. The group was to include his mother, his brother, John, his wife and three children. Susanna, his sister, who lived nearby also decided to move in with her husband and their sixteen children. The Family Ferrar which now planned to descend on the tiny hamlet numbered almost thirty persons. Later, when they invited some nearby widows to live with them, the number would grow to forty.

Before any of this could take place, however, the plague struck London with a vengeance. It arrived in March, 1626, a year after King James died and Charles had succeeded him. First, a neighbor next door to the Ferrar's home in London died and several members of the family attended the funeral. When another neighbor died, Nicholas realizing the danger to which the family had been exposed, quickly ordered his mother and his brother, John and family, to his sister's home in Bourne Bridge.

The plague quickly became a major catastrophe—claiming four thousand victims a week with more than that number fleeing the city. Nicholas now decided it was time for him to leave. But instead of going to his sister's house, he went straight to Little Gidding to quarantine himself from his family for a month or so, to avoid the possibility of infecting them.

* * * * *

Appalled by these events, I decided to return to the tiny hamlet and attempt to visualize what it must have been like for Nicholas to arrive at Little Gidding after fleeing the awful terrors of London. Upon my arrival I sat for awhile in the small church and pondered the situation.

While I sat ruminating on how difficult it must have been to live in those dreadful days, I noticed the figure of a small, elderly woman sitting on the bench near the front of the church. She must have been very attractive as a young woman because age had treated her kindly. She sat very erect, quietly watching me. Thinking I had blundered upon her devotions, I hurriedly rose to excuse myself. She raised her hand.

"Do not leave, young man, I came to tell you what it was like."

I stared at her.

"Yes, my dear man, I am Mary Ferrar, Nicholas's mother."

"What you have been reading is all true. Nicholas had urged me not to come but I was impatient to see him so I borrowed one of my daughter's horses and rode through the muddy roads and fields to get here. Nicholas, while very glad to see me, chided me for being so foolish to attempt such a journey at my age. But I would have none of it. I told him I wanted to be sure he was taken care of, and that my curiosity about the condition of this place had gotten the best of me. So I just had to come."

"I was aghast at the condition of the buildings, especially the small church. It had been used as a barn by a nearby farmer. The chancel had been a pig-sty; and hay had been stored in the rest of the building. There was no glass left in the windows; the woodwork was rotting and decayed; the floor was littered with every kind of filth and rubbish. Imagine! This had been a church for almost five hundred years and for several centuries had been under the patronage of the Crown and it had been abused in such terrible ways. I was scandalized. I insisted that Nicholas have the workmen he'd hired to work on the house immediately begin cleaning out and purifying this temple of the Lord."

"For some time, I stayed on alone with Nicholas. He

supervised the cleaning of the house while I gave my full attention to the repair and cleaning of the church. After a time, when Nicholas felt the danger from the plague had passed, we invited the rest of the family to join us. It took me almost two years to restore the church. A new floor and wainscotting had to be installed throughout. The communion table was placed on a raised half-step. It was made of cedar wood and stood upon a carpet of blue silk embroidered in gold. A new pulpit and reading desk was purchased and hung with fine blue cloth with a valance of silk lace. Benches were installed on either side of the central aisle, much like is seen in a college chapel. They were backed with blue taffeta and the cushions were covered with tapestry and blue silk with silver fringes. My daughters and I enjoyed doing the needlework to make this holy sanctuary a worthy place to worship the Lord."

"Perhaps you may not believe this, but the ancient brass baptismal font had been used by the farmer for the watering of his calves. We had it thoroughly scrubbed and polished and set it in place by the pulpit. A friend of mine in France found a centuries old brass lectern with a huge eagle adorning it and promptly bought it for me."

"And, oh yes, I failed to mention what I did with the space behind the communion table. It was stunning. The wainscotting was made of the most beautiful wood. Then, on four tablets of brass gilt I had engraved the Ten Commandments, the Lord's Prayer and the Apostle's Creed. The communion table itself was furnished with a silver patin, a silver chalice and silver candlesticks with large wax candles placed in them. Similar candles were placed in every part of the church and upon all the posts of the stalls. They were placed there for light, you know, not for superstitous purposes."

"Finally, because of my love for music I had a gallery constructed at the back of the church for an organ."

She hesitated, and I could not be sure if she was about to leave me as the other ghosts had done. Instead, she sat very silently, apparently lost in thought. After a moment, she continued.

"I failed to mention that above the altar table, that had been placed in a position to please the Bishop, we had installed three plain glass windows with bars to protect them. The bars had no other significance."

"Nicholas later told me the Bishop or his surrogate, I forget which, suggested we install a painted glass window and in it a crucifix, but that he had refused."

"In all of this, I thought, nay believed," Mary continued, *"that we were preparing a suitable sanctuary in which to worship Our Lord. For this reason, I had a plaque mounted above the fireplace in the house. It was very plain with a christian symbol displayed above a suitable message welcoming all who came to visit us in Christian love."*

She sighed with a sadness that tore at my heart, then said slowly, "I never realized that my handiwork would ever lead to such terrible consequences. . . ."

I stared at her, not comprehending but keeping silent.

After awhile, she continued.

"I know that you have speculated as to why my son, Nicholas, gave up a brilliant career to retire from the world. You seemed to have guessed the two most important reasons. It is true that he felt he had only a short time to live on this earth and, further, he was close enough to events of the time to know that terrible things were about to happen. I always felt from the time he was a little boy that he had a special gift. Why, even when he was traveling in Europe he sensed something was wrong at home before we even wrote about it."

Mary's comment reminded me of the trance Nicholas Ferrar reported having in Europe when he dreamed he was desperately needed at home.

I realized she had not stopped speaking to me!

" . . . *we were apart from the world here in Little Gidding, but we were still very much in the midst of the religious turmoil. Even the beautiful work we did in this sanctuary was not safe. The lovely blue cloth with gold and silver trimming was stolen from the church one night. Later, thieves were found with it on them, much torn and mangled. You will not believe it when I tell you, too, that there was even much controversy about the position of the communion—or altar table—which I'd had especially made for the church. The controversy was over its position on the chancel! Oh, I am certain you will discover much about Little Gidding and this church that was misunderstood and hatefully reported. It caused much heartache and misery. But we were not alone in that; it was happening all over England.*"

Her voice became weak and I worried that the effort was tiring her. It was.

"My dear man, I have told you all that I am able to tell. I came to Little Gidding when I was over seventy years of age. My life here for eight years was one of joy and fulfillment. I had no regrets when my life on earth ended in peace. I had not even lost a tooth, nor showed one sign of age. I feel as St. Paul did, that I 'kept the faith, fought the good fight, and stayed the course;' no one can ask more . . ."

On that note, Mary Ferrar vanished from my sight. But somehow I sensed she would always be close at hand whenever I came to the little church.

Nicholas's mother had filled in some of the details about Little Gidding but she left me with several unanswered questions. Unfortunately, many of Nicholas Ferrar's original papers have mysteriously disappeared but many of his letters and other papers are to be found in the library at Magdalene College, Cambridge University. While they shed much light on his life and the life of the community at Little Gidding, they are often contradictory.

Most of the factual details about the life of the community, however, seem quite straightforward. When Nicholas decided to retire, he became a deacon of the Church of England so he could provide spiritual leadership for the group. The routines of the household that he set appear to be a direct throwback to the daily regime followed by the Knights and their families who lived at the preceptory centuries earlier. A typical day began before dawn to hear Matins; followed by morning chores; Bible study (the children reading the psalms aloud). The meals were simple: breakfast was bread and coffee; lunch a meatless meal. In the afternoon, the entire household observed Vespers followed by supper; before retiring everyone assembled for an evening service after which orders for the next day were issued.

One major difference from the routine of centuries earlier appears to be a daily procession to the church with Nicholas bringing up the rear clad in surplice, hood and square cap, and escorting his mother. Upon entering the church the entire group touched a knee to the floor before sitting. Nicholas conducted the service except on Sunday when the rector of the church at Great Gidding—a mile away—came to the community to officiate at the service.

The household and other chores were in many respects similar to the earlier preceptories with the women doing the household chores, and the men performing other duties both in and around the house and on the farm. Within a year's time widows in the nearby community were invited to come and live at Little Gidding. (This, too, may have happened during the time of the Crusades when women would be widowed by slain Knights.) A school for small children of the household and nearby neigbors was soon established, as was an infirmary to care for members of the household and neighbors.

Several members of the family undertook to learn the art of bookbinding. This entailed gilding, lettering, something called pasting-printing, and the use of the rolling press. These skills were almost entirely directed at producing Bible concordances of such distinction and beauty they soon attracted the attention of King Charles and his family. It was a mundane activity but its consequences for the community and church would be enormous.

All of these activities appear quite in keeping with a group that had decided to dedicate itself to a life of service to God and man. But the times were quite out of joint, and any activity of a religious nature by one group caused suspicion by another group. Consequently, it was not long before rumors were abroad about the happenings at Little Gidding. People far and wide began to overtly and covertly visit the place. In the beginning, the household heartily greeted everyone with cordiality and a meal. But as rumors spread and the country was torn by religious and political strife, Nicholas and his mother became increasingly wary of visitors. Soon, only persons who appeared in need of a hot meal were welcomed. However, persons of an inquisitive nature discovered this ploy and began dressing like tramps to gain entrance to the house.

In 1634, two events happened which in later years would prove disastrous. King Charles, who appears to have kept in touch with Nicholas after he moved to the country, heard of a project Nicholas had completed and printed. It was called the Gidding Gospel Harmony, a single account compiled from the four Gospels and illustrated by pictures gathered by Nicholas during his travels in Europe. The King, who was staying at nearby Apethorpe, sent a messenger requesting the book for several days.

Several months later, Charles, who had kept the book, sent word that he was using it daily and would return it on the condition they make him another copy he could keep. This new copy took a year to complete, and when the

King received it he was so overjoyed that he promptly re-
quested they compile another harmony of other books of
Holy Scripture for him. This Nicholas agreed to do, and for
the project he selected two books of the Old Testament,
Kings and Chronicles. In due time, this project was completed and duly presented to His Majesty, who expressed
keen delight with it.

In the same year that this happened, 1634, a barrister by the name of Edward Lenton personally appeared at
Little Gidding to inquire about rumors of the place that
were common currency even in London. Just why he had
taken it upon himself to do so, and why he wrote a detailed
letter of his visit and sent copies to several of his friends
but did not bother to send one to Nicholas Ferrar, remains a
mystery. Of interest, too, is that it would later be used as
the basis for a malicious and incendiary document about
the community at Little Gidding.

The letter is one of those historical gems which survive from time to time not only to titillate the historian, but
more important to shed light on otherwise confusing data.
Further, it was written by a person with an extraordinarily
observant eye, who used a lawyer's skill at cross examining
people—seeming to remain both understanding of what
they were telling him but skeptical at their response.

As I sat in the church reading a copy of the letter
which had surfaced in 1730, one hundred years after it had
been written, I realized the letter fitted the context of my
earlier conversations with the ghosts of Little Gidding so I
decided to convert it into a conversation between Edward
Lenton, the barrister, and Nicholas Ferrar, the deacon.

The letter, itself, opens with an explanation by Mr.
Lenton that he was visiting Little Gidding because it was
reported (or at least reputed) to be a nunnery. Following fa-
vorable comments on the house and the condition of the
grounds, he enters the house and is greeted by Nicholas
Ferrar who insists he meet his aged Mother; his older brother, John; his sister, Susanna; and a young man whose appa-
rel and hairstyle he describes "as almost priestlike." Lenton
then writes,

"I saluted the Mother and daughter, not like nuns, but as we salute other women."

Following this opening he engages Nicholas in a conversation, which with very little change in substance follows:

Lenton: *"I first want to tell you I have heard of two nuns of Gidding; of watching and praying all night; of canonical hours; of crosses on the outside and inside of the church; of an altar there that is richly decked with plate; also elegant tapestry; many tapers; and of your adorations and geniculations at your entering therein."*

Nicholas, cutting him off, *"I protest the implication that this is a 'papist' place; I do verily believe the pope to be an anti-Christ. As for the nunnery, I consider that designation odious. The truth is that two of my nieces, one thirty, the other thirty-two, are virgins and are resolved to continue to be so, the better to give themselves to fasting and prayer. But that is all."*
"As for the canonical hours, we usually pray six times a day, twice in the church, and four times privately in the house. In the church we pray after the order of the book of common prayer; in the house, we pray particular prayers meant for a private family."

Lenton: *"So much time spent in prayer would seem to leave little time for preaching or doing your regular chores. I recall the Bible cautions us that 'He that turneth away his ear from hearing the law, even his prayer shall be an abomination.' Also, another text states: 'Six days shalt thou labor . . . ' "*

Nicholas: *"The rector from Gidding comes to preach on Sunday mornings, sometimes we go there to hear* *him. Further, we believe our calling is to serve God as best we can."*

Lenton: *"Some people believe that for healthy, active folk to quit their calling and spend their lives fasting, praying and contemplating is little better than a serious kind of idleness."*

Nicholas: *"We found nothing but many perplexities, distractions and almost utter ruin in our callings. But if people knew the comfort and contentment God has given us in our sequestration they might be encouraged to follow us!"*

Lenton: *"For your night watching and for rising every morning at four, it must be difficult for you and your Mother, at her age."*

Nicholas: *"The early risings are not difficult, as she and I retire at seven every evening. For the night vigils, I confess we take turns; several stay up praying and then go to bed when the others arise."*

Lenton: *"What about the rumors of the many crosses in the house and church."*

Nicholas: *"We are not ashamed of that badge of Christ which the first occupants of this place wore on their mantles and banners."*

Lenton: *"I note that it is now near eleven—your chapel time; might I accompany you there and satisfy myself best of what I heard concerning that? In the meantime, I have satisfied myself that all was not true of what I had heard of this place, except for the inscription on the frontispiece of the house containing a strange invitation for the* *curious who visited here. As yet I have not seen it."*

Nicholas: *"The inscription is just above your head over the fireplace."*

Lenton, after reading it: *"I crave to beg leave to copy it."*

Nicholas Ferrar forthwith took down the inscribed plaque and told the young man with the long hair to make a copy of it. When Edward Lenton offered to pay for it the young man refused to accept his money, and Nicholas insisted that Lenton not offer to pay for anything in the house.

Lenton then made a copy of the inscription which reads as follows:

IHS

He that by reproof of our errors or Remonstrance of that which is more perfect, seeks to make us better, is welcome as an angel of God

He that any way goes about to divert or disturb us in that which is as it ought to be among Christians, though it be not usual in the world, is a burthen whilst he stays, and shall bear his judgement whosoever he be.

He that by a cheerful participating in that which is good confirms us in the same is welcome as a Christian Friend.

But

He that faults us in absence for that which in presence he made show to approve shall by a double guilt of flattery and slander violate the bands both of Friendship [and] Christianity.

Mary Ferrar widow
Mother of this Family
And aged about Fourscore years
That bids adieu to all fears and hopes of this world and only
desires to serve God.

Lenton, after copying the inscription, looks up at Nicholas with a puzzled expression on his face.

Lenton: *"But if you will beg my pardon, I believe the initials over the inscription are used by every Jesuit in every book and exhibit of theirs."*

Nicholas retorts: *"The Jesuits are an auspicious name. Also, the Holy Scripture commands us to write such things on the posts of our houses and upon our gates. I refer you to Deuteronomy, Chapter 6, verse 9."*

Lenton: *"I am far from excepting of the sacred name of Jesus but I believe the Chapter and Verse of the Scripture to which you refer makes no mention of Jesus; it refers to Jehovah."*

Nothing further being said of the above, and after they were served refreshments by a maid, **Lenton** then describes what happened when they entered the church.

"At the entering he, Nicholas, made a low obeisance; a few paces further, a lower; coming to the half-pace (chancel) he bowed to the ground, if not prostrated himself; then went up into a fair, large reading place (a preaching place of some proportion, right over against it). The Mother with all her train (which were her daughter and her daughter's daughters) had a fair island seat. He placed me above, on the half-pace, with two fair window cushions of green velvet before me. The children were all in black except the daughter's daughter who was in a friar's grey gown.
"We thus being placed, Nicholas began the Litany, read divers prayers and collects in the Book of Common-prayer, the Athanasius' Creed, and concluded with the 'Peace of God'; etc."

After the family departed from the church, Lenton was left alone with Nicholas to observe the church at his leisure. He commented on the herbs and flowers, the large tapers on every post, the half-pace or altar and the nave all covered with tapestry. He noted that on the altar stood a communion table on a rich carpet, adorned with silver plate, a chalice and some candlesticks with wax candles.

Lenton then asks Nicholas, *"Why so many candles?"*

Nicholas responds, *"To give us light. We could not see without them."*

Lenton then asks him, *"To whom do you make so many obeisances?"*

Nicholas responds, *"To God."*

Lenton: *"For those papists who bow to images and crucifixes, we call them idolaters for so doing."*

Nicholas: *"We have no warrant for the first but for the second, I refer you to I Corinthians 14:40."*

Lenton: *"Since you do not use such solemnity in the house, do you consider the church more holy than the house?"*

Nicholas: *"No. But God is more immediately present while we are worshipping Him in His temple."*

Lenton: *"I thought God was present outside of St. Paul's church as well as inside. We are taught, 'Where two or three are gathered together in His Name, God is in the midst of them'."*

Lenton writes in his letter at this point that he either did not understand Nicholas's answer or did not hear it.

At this point the letter ends, and Lenton calls for his horse to make his departure. He does note he had hoped he would be invited to stay for dinner. He closes the letter by commenting on the good works of the community. How they help the poor and the sick, etc. Then he explains that while he challenged some of Nicholas's opinions and practices only by *"way of argument, and for my own better information . . . I found them (all) full of humanity and humility."*

As we shall soon see, this seemingly innocent letter, much to the dismay of its author, would inflame the Parliament and the entire countryside against Little Gidding. But there are two aspects of it which deserve comment before proceeding further. It is apparent that with all the disagreements over worship and ritual, the matter of doctrine seems never to have been in question. Lenton's letter, however it was used, makes not the slightest mention of faith or beliefs —it is all about form. Second, the reference to the Jesuits is very puzzling. In Queen Elizabeth's time, there was no doubt the Jesuits were sent into England to bring that nation back into the Roman Catholic Church under the Pope. A history of the Society of Jesus, their official name, written as recently as 1982, refers to them by the designation, 'His Holiness's Secret Service.' Further, the notes of Nicholas's travels abroad are from a book written in 1907, and appear to be his personal comments. They clearly indicate that he was very wary, even fearful, of the Jesuits when he was in Rome and other Catholic countries. Lenton's reference to Nicholas's reply to the inscription on the plaque over the fireplace in the house, which Mary Ferrar's spirit alluded to, is puzzling in light of those-experiences.

A current guide to Little Gidding, by the present rector of the church, contends that Nicholas Ferrar was eager to maintain contact "with the Roman Catholic community in England, (but) it was too dangerous for Catholic priests and Jesuits to stay at Little Gidding, so he had them housed at Leighton Bromswold, a small village five miles from Little Gidding, and discreetly brought them to Little Gidding . . . in hopes of finding common ground . . . ."

When one considers the temper of those times, this appears to be both a contradiction and a foolhardy activity for Nicholas. It is, however, important to recognize that the religious conflict was not between some wild, uneducated, illiterate people from the mountains, but between men and women who were intelligent, educated people so embued with their own concepts of the Christian church, they had lost their way.

An example of this is found in the Church of England itself. The fight over vestments and the episcopacy had become so virulent that little or no attention was paid to the liturgy of the church service. Nicholas Ferrar is credited by many church scholars with trying to correct this oversight. A fact that has been largely overlooked in the history of the period. Then, too, it is possible that he was using his considerable talents by engaging in conversations with the Catholic clergy in an attempt to head off the confrontation between religious factions that he sensed was about to envelope the nation. But we get ahead of our story.

* * * * *

Not too long after the visit from Edward Lenton, Mary Ferrar died. At the time, she could not know that the wonderful work she had accomplished in repairing the church and installing a simple plaque over the fireplace at the house at Little Gidding would bring such terrible times to her beloved homestead. (From my conversation with her spirit, though, she obviously had become very much aware of the calamities that befell the place!)

It was three years later, in 1637, that the fates of the three men, Nicholas, Oliver and Charles, would begin to be inexorably intertwined with that of the community. Whether it was fate or just plain fecklessness, their careers so obviously different began moving them and England toward an inevitable and inconceivable climax.

For his part, Nicholas had been immensely pleased by the interest that King Charles had shown in his efforts to rearrange the books of the Bible. He now conceived an idea for a project to be used as a gift to present to the Prince of Wales, named Charles, after his father, the King. The book would be centered on what Nicholas described as "the whole law of God" which he believed was to be found in the five books of Moses. Further, the Scriptures would be placed under an elaborate pattern of headings that would serve to harmonize the prophesies about Jesus that are found in the Old Testament.

Alas, before the year was out, Nicholas health failed and he died on December 4, 1637, at 1:00 A. M.—the exact hour at which he had always risen to begin his prayers. The evening before he died Nicholas held a last conversation with his brother, John, in which he signalled what was to come. Although his papers have been lost to us, what he said to his brother at that time has been recorded in several histories of the period.

"I now tell you, that you may be forewarned and prepare for it, there will be sad times come, and very sad; you will live to see them, but be courageous, and hold you fast to God with humility and patience, rely upon His mercy and power; you will suffer much, but God will help you; and endeavor will be made to turn you out of the right way, the good way you are in, even by those whom you least think of, and your troubles will be many; but be you stead-fast, and call upon God, and He in His good and due time will help you. Ah, my brother, my brother, I pity you, I pity your case and what you may live to see, even with great al-terations. God will bring punishments upon this land, but, I trust not to the utter ruin of it . . . . "

Nicholas Ferrar was never more prescient than just before he passed away. As we shall soon see, dark days were about to enshroud Little Gidding. The Arminian Nunnery would be created in the minds of some people; his brother, John, would become embroiled in a plot to help King Charles that would almost destroy him and the community at Little Gidding; and all of England would live a nightmare for the next twenty one years.

For his part, King Charles made 1637 an eventful one for himself and for England and Scotland as well. His royal proclamation that the English Book of Common Prayer be used in all church services in Scotland was carried out for the first time that year in St. Giles Cathedral, Edinburgh. The reaction of the Scots was swift and violent. Within months, the Scottish Presbyterians drew up a National Covenant which swore to defend the true religion— Presbyterianism—in "Kirk and Kingdom." By 1638, all of the rituals and institutions which Charles and his Archbishops had been trying to impose on Scotland were wiped out.

The beleaguered King now made a fateful decision: he decided to raise an army and force the rituals and the Prayer Book on the Scots by force. His first attempt failed miserably, probably because the King listened to his wife's advice and tried to use Catholic troops subsidized by her French father and the Pope. Undaunted, the King now hastily organized an English army to force his wishes on the Scots. This effort failed, too. The enterprise lacked two ingredients necessary to any successful military enterprise: discipline and money. And so this First Bishop's War, as it was called, ended in a truce between the Scots and the English. Charles agreed to call a new General Assembly in Scotland and agreed that it exclude all Bishops!

But the King was not as yet ready to give in or give up. When the General Assembly did not produce what he desired, he decided to recall Parliament. They had not held a session in eleven years but Charles was in desperate need of money.

*　*　*　*　*

While King Charles was so stubbornly engaged in imposing his will on the people of Scotland, Oliver Crom-

well was experiencing his own grief with the kind of pre-
science that inhabited the psyche of Nicholas Ferrar. His
wife, Elizabeth, having given birth to her ninth and last
child, died at forty years of age. His eldest son, Robert,
died of a mysterious, rapidly developing fever which decimated so many English homes at that time. Oliver bespoke
of his shattering grief and of a blackness which had descended upon him—further evidence of the fits of melan-
choly that would beset him all of his life. He now believed
that his future was governed by Divine Will over which he
had no control. Also, that what he had been taught as a
child at the feet of a stern Puritan teacher—that God was a
harsh God—was proving to be true. It would be these two
concepts that would govern the rest of his life. And so it
was, that a despondent Oliver Cromwell returned to Parliament that in his desperation, King Charles had summoned.

Oliver just ignored the King's plea for funds to pursue his war against the Scots, and gave his full attention to
a document produced by the Archbishop of Canterbury,
Bishop Laud. At the urging of King Charles, Bishop Laud
had drawn up a list of religious innovations which included
such ideas as universal suspension of penal laws against
Catholics, church ceremonies which included bowing (genuflecting) to the altar, even a Papal nuncio appointed to the
Court (probably Henrietta's idea), and, from Oliver Cromwell's point of view at least, the most devastating of all,
was the concept that Divine Will was bestowed by God
only upon the Bishops of the Church of England. When a
prominent and outspoken leader of Parliament, John Pym,
characterized these innovations as nothing less than a pop-
ish plot, Oliver agreed.

For his part, Charles was equally aghast to find he
could not count on the natural enmity which existed between the English people and the Scottish people to fuel his
war! Within three weeks he again dissolved the Parliament.
This time he decided to use instead a convocation of clergy
to carry out his purpose. They did so in a strange way by
providing him with six subsidies, or benevolences as they
termed them, to support another army to fight the Scots.

This was called the Second Bishop's War and it, too, ended in defeat for King Charles. The resultant treaty, known as the treaty of Ripon, added a new dimension of ignominy to Charles's efforts. This time the Scottish soldiers who remained behind on English soil were to receive a subsidy of 850 pounds a day until a final settlement to the war could be reached!

The violent reaction against this by the English was so strong, Charles was forced against his will to again recall Parliament. For yet another time, the members returned but this time brooding revenge. Among them was an even angrier Oliver Cromwell. To the astonishment of the Ferrar family at Little Gidding, as each member of Parliament returned to Parliament and entered the building, he was handed a pamphlet entitled, "The Arminian Nunnery." It was a subtle and damaging re-write of the letter Edward Lenton had written to a friend some years earlier reporting on his visit to Little Gidding.

The title, the sketches of the church, and the text of the pamphlet virtually inflamed the already angry members of Parliament. The cover of the publication displayed a woman dressed as a nun holding a rosary. In the background, a crude drawing showed a church topped by a round tower (much like the earlier churches of the Knights Templar). Under the title was a sub-head which read "A brief description of the late erected Monasticall (sic) Place called Little Gidding."

The text of the pamphlet played on such things as the inscription over the front door of the house which Mary Ferrar had placed there as a pointed reminder to visitors as to why they came and what was expected of them. It then placed great stress on "the genuflecting at the altar in the church—the members crouching, cringing and prostrating to the ground to the altar-like communion table . . . ;" and "the priest-like pregnant proculator" (a reference to Nicholas Ferrar); "the monastic setting of the community; the crosses and the superstitious nunneries (such as) exist beyond the seas . . . . "

One of the most damaging references concerned the

Jesuits. The pamphlet pointed out that "the letters (IHS) above the inscription were "the proper characters of the Jesuits in every book and exhibit of theirs." (Ed. Note. The letters IHS are an abbreviation of a Greek word meaning "Jesus," and have been identified with the Society of Jesus since its founding by St. Ignatius in the 14th Century. Further, it should be recalled that the ghost of Mary Ferrar referred to the inscription as nothing more than "a simple christian symbol.")

The reference to the Jesuits appears to have caused most of the uproar among the members of Parliament. However, a reference to "the crosses on the windows," reveals the deep feelings against religious symbols which existed especially among the Puritan members. The windows and the crosses referred to in the pamphlet were the plain glass windows over the altar which were held in place by three upright iron and four horizontal bars. To a suspicious mind the iron bars would appear to be crosses. The pamphlet clearly intended to convey the thought that the people at Little Gidding were engaged in genuflecting to these "crosses" when they approached the altar.

John Ferrar, Nicholas' brother, later estimated that over nine thousand of these pamphlets were, over time, printed and distributed even to the members of the Army, later commanded by Oliver Cromwell.

The phrase "Arminian Nunnery," used as the title for the pamphlet was particularly galling to the Puritans: those who wanted to reform the Church of England and those who opposed outright the Catholic Church and its complete obedience to the Pope in Rome. "Arminianism," as it was called had become quite popular in England among many clergy and Bishops of the Church. As earlier mentioned it referred to a concept developed by a Dutch theologian in Leyden by the name of Arminius, who taught that man was saved by good works but that mankind itself had no individual liberty and therefore must give full obedience to the King. The Puritans who believed in free will under God, felt that "Arminianism" was a not so subtle "bridge to Popery" and completely rejected it. Thus, Little

Gidding quickly became known as The Arminian Nunnery: a scandalously "secret" Catholic establishment which sheltered nuns; conducted strange religious services, and followed peculiar practices in a strange church completely cut off from the rest of the world around it.

Incredibly, the small community now became a lightening rod for the friction between the King and his subjects over religious issues. The issues on all sides seemed centered around symbols and forms of worship rather than its substance. A condition more aptly described, if you will, as Churchianity not Christianity.

It was into this incendiary and fateful situation that the Parliament called by King Charles now reconvened. When it did, the religious turmoil boiled over and engulfed the entire nation. In rapid succession, the House of Commons received: 1) a resolution excoriating "The Arminian Nunnery;" 2) impeachment proceedings against Bishop Laud (a friend of Little Gidding) on the grounds of "popery and treason;" and, 3) petitions from Oliver Cromwell, among others, requesting that Parliament abolish all Bishops and restore the government of the church to the people. These petitions put forth the claim that many Bishops of the Church of England did not affirm the Pope as Anti-Christ as most members of Parliament thought they should. For his part, Oliver Cromwell went even further; he charged that the Bishops secretly subscribed to the doctrine that the way to salvation came only through the Catholic Church and thus the Pope. This, he declared was repugnant to him, and to all his fellow Puritans.

Although there is no record of the action taken by Parliament on the resolution about "The Arminian Nunnery," history does record that Bishop Laud was impeached and later executed. Further, the petitions so wholeheartedly supported by Cromwell were rejected. Instead, the House of Commons voted simply to disbar all clergy from any further legislative and judicial functions. For its part, the House of Lords agreed but insisted that the Bishops be allowed to remain in their places in that body.

Three years later, in 1641, Oliver Cromwell again

proposed the total abolition of all Bishops. When the House
of Commons passed it but the House of Lords rejected it,
Commons reacted by resolving that all scandalous pictures
of the Trinity, all images of the Virgin Mary, all crosses
and superstitious figures be removed from all English
churches. Although the House of Lords rejected that propo-
sal out of hand, the idea swept England and chaos among
the religious houses followed. Altar rails and screens were
torn down; stained glass windows smashed; statues demol-
ished; religious pictures cut to shreds. Hostile crowds now
prevented the Bishops from even gaining entrance to Parliament. King Charles was beside himself. He swore that he
would die rather than give in but eventually he did both.

Seemingly, without let-up, the troubles between the
King and Parliament continued to grow until the nation was
divided into two camps: those favoring the transference of
all power, religious and otherwise, from the King to Parliament; and those who opposed any further diminution in the
powers of the Crown. But, as so often happens in the affairs
of nations, people on either side had now become so committed, they feared for their own safety. Oliver Cromwell,
for one, now felt his life was in jeopardy if King Charles
should recover his full power. At one time, Oliver even
toyed with the idea of emigrating to America where tens of
thousands of his fellow Puritans now lived. Finally, decid-
ing to remain in England, he became convinced that King
Charles would use his Catholic wife, Henrietta, to persuade
the Catholic Army from Ireland to invade England.

In the middle of all this, Little Gidding was again
thrust into the nation's consciousness in the strangest of
ways. Instead of dissolving Parliament, as he had again
threatened, King Charles left London to travel north to
York to rally support for his views from that part of the
country. On the way, he happened to pass close to the small
community, and seeing it, decided to pay it a visit and inquire about the project Nicholas Ferrar had begun just before he died.

How unreal this seems. His nation was on the verge
of civil war, yet the King of England with the Great Seal in

his possession for safety's sake took time for a leisurely stop at a little community to spend the afternoon looking into a Bible project. To be sure his wife, Henrietta, was not with him. She had taken it upon herself to flee England for France secretly taking the Crown Jewels of England with her!

Undoubtedly, King Charles was keenly interested in the Bible project because of his knowledge of Nicholas Ferrar's earlier work, but during his visit he also showed a great curiosity about things that had caused the community such notoriety when the members of Parliament saw the pamphlet about "The Arminian Nunnery." The records of his visit, which exist today in the London Museum, reveal that he was interested in the inscription over the front door of the house and examined it carefully. Also, that he visited the small church and asked many questions about the furnishings, the window, worship services and the like. Obviously, he had studied the pamphlet very closely.

There is one other feature of his visit which holds some significance for a later event that would further ensnare the community. As he was leaving, the King asked to see John Ferrar privately and engaged him in a lengthy discussion, the substance of which was never recorded.

While Charles was thus engaged, back in London the Parliament ordered all armed forces to obey only those orders issued by it and not those of the King. This action prompted a number of members of both Houses to quit Parliament, leave London, and join the King in his northern retreat. To strenthen its power with the people, those who remained in Parliament justified their action by stating they had taken such drastic action because they expected an uprising of the Catholics in England that would result in a massacre of Puritans!

For his part, Oliver Cromwell now decided to leave London and return to his own county, Huntingdonshire, not too many miles from Little Gidding, to organize the defenses of his own community. The forces he now organized would later become known as "The Ironsides," a nickname that would stick to Oliver Cromwell for the rest of his life.

But while Oliver was at home, an incident occurred involving John Ferrar which again cast Little Gidding in a bad light. (The groundwork may have been laid when King Charles visited the community and held his private conversation with John, but no record exists of the substance of that conversation.) What is known is that Charles, in desperate need of money, had secretly appealed for help wherever he could obtain it. A group of his supporters at Cambridge now decided to use the silver plate from the college dining rooms to help him. John Ferrar was one of those engaged in attempting to spirit the plate into the hands of the King's supporters! The plot, if it could be called such, was unearthed by none other than Oliver Cromwell. The silver was recovered, and apparently all of the conspirators escaped unharmed.

The incident at Cambridge, though, does reveal one of the strangest dichotomies ever to befall a nation. England was now divided: politically, economically and religously, but not in the ways one would think. London and the port cities, the manufacturing towns in the south, and most of the new middle class were practically all Puritans who supported the Parliament. On the other hand, the two universities, Cambridge and Oxford, the towns to the west and the north, most of the aristocrats plus the landed gentry supported the King.

It was spring when King Charles made his fateful visit to Little Gidding; by summer of that year, 1642, Civil War broke out all over England. Charles left the north and returned to Oxford to be joined by his wife who now brought arms and ammunition plus the Crown Jewels to aid his cause. It was now Parliament's turn to need help as the King had done previously. It, too, turned to Scotland for help. Not surprisingly, the Scots set a price on their participation—a religious one: Both England and Ireland would be required to become Presbyterian and all church government was to be ruled by presbyteries and not by the King, Parliament or even the Bishops.

When Charles heard this, he immediately sought peace with Irish resurgents and tried to bring them to England to fight on his side against both the English Puritans and the Scottish Presbyterians. The Anglicans and the Catholics were delighted; the Puritans were even angrier than before. So the English Civil War now involved not only England but Scotland and Ireland and not only Puritans and Presbyterians but Anglicans and Catholics: three nations and four faiths! Small wonder so many people of all religious persuasions, but especially the Puritans, continued to flee to America.

Over the next several years, while the King's fortunes were in steady decline, Oliver Cromwell's were steadily rising. Not only did he demonstrate exceptional skill at soldiering, he was now made Governor of Isle of Ely, and was even closer to Little Gidding than before. He used the position to assert his religious preferences. while giving license to all new religious sects, he suppressed the Anglican service in the Cathedral of Ely and ended any singing for the next sixteen years.

There is scant evidence to show what was happening at the community which Nicholas Ferrar had started so reverently and with such high ideals just twenty years before. But there can be little doubt that it was left unscathed. There is evidence that the sacking of churches was happening all over that part of England. One group of Cromwell's army—he had now risen to a high command of the troops—is said to have desecrated the great Peterborough Cathedral, a scant twelve miles north of Little Gidding.

When the King's forces were defeated at nearby Naseby and Charles sought sanctuary at Oxford, the families remaining at Little Gidding were in mortal terror. Indeed, John Ferrar tried to place the community in a more positive light in the public's eye. The records show he implored several friends to place on exhibit some of the religious works printed at Little Gidding so the world might come to recognize the community as a place for contemplation and not religious chicanery. But the King's fortunes were now swiftly ebbing and the kind of help or support Little Gidding hoped for was not forthcoming. But, strangely enough, it was not long before Charles would again enter the life of the tiny community and unfortunately bring it more grief.

But before recounting that part of the story, another strange occurrence needs be mentioned. Earlier, in describing Little Gidding, I pointed out that over the entrance to the church is the biblical reference from the book of Genesis: "This is None Other Than The House of God and the Gate of Heaven." History records that after the victory at Naseby which ended the First Civil War in English history and eventually forced the King to flee for his life, Oliver Cromwell, in rejoicing at the victory, used the same biblical reference but altered it to fit his own situation by declaring of the victory: "This is None Other Than The Hand of God . . .!"

But stranger things were yet to happen and the tiny community would once again be in the middle. With the city of Oxford now under siege by the forces of Parliament, Charles, who had sought refuge there, escaped in disguise. This time he was not accompanied by his son and a retinue of attendants, but by two men who were destined to meet with violent ends. It was in early spring of 1646, and the King and his two companions appear to have traveled laterally across the Midlands of England to Norfolk, and then in a north and westerly direction so as to skirt Cambridge and Ely. This brought them close to Little Gidding, at which point they seemed to have parted company because at nightfall on May 2, 1646, King Charles, to the surprise of everyone at the community, appeared at the door alone seeking refuge.

John Ferrar received His Majesty with all respect, but immediately advised him that Little Gidding was no longer a safe place, least of all for the King. He told Charles that the community was now suspect even by its neighbors, and that soldiers from the army now led by Cromwell were known to be in the vicinity. In one of the strangest, most poignant stories in English history, John Ferrar in the dark of the night with only a candle to guide them accompanied the King of England across the fields to the safety of a nearby farmer's house; one who was known

to support the Crown. It was there that King Charles—
alone, dispirited and afraid—spent the rest of the night. The
next morning he continued on his journey north, stopping at
the town of Stamford, several miles from Little Gidding.

Would that this story about a King and a small community of faith giving succor to a King could end at this
point. But it does not. It was not too many days after the
event that word reached Cromwell that the King had been
seen either entering or leaving Little Gidding. Whether a
suspicious neighbor or a soldier saw King Charles enter
and leave the community is not known. What is known, is
that within days soldiers of the army led by Cromwell resolved to plunder the community. The family, being informed of their hasty approach, thought it prudent to flee at
once. In a rage, the soldiers forthwith proceeded to ransack
first the church and then the house. The organ reportedly
was smashed to pieces and used to make a large bonfire.
Several of the Ferrars's sheep were killed and roasted over
the fire. This done, the soldiers seized all the silver, furni-
ture and provisions which they conveniently carried away.
Some of Nicholas Ferrar's work was destroyed in the general devastation.

The family members and the other inhabitants of the
community fled for their lives. Where they went no one
seems to know. They returned in the summer of 1647 when
it seemed, for a little while, that King Charles and the Parliament would come to terms and a normal life might return
to England. A phrase in one of the letters found among the
archives vividly expresses the feeling of unease that existed
among the members of Little Gidding at the time, "All
things at this time are in so dubious a calm, that fear is
greatest when the danger is less."

PERSPECTIVES FROM VIRGINIA

Several years passed before I returned to Little Gidding to continue my research. Its troubled past, the part it played in the dark days of English history, and the way the careers of three men of such differing backgrounds and beliefs had converged on the small community had saddened me. I was not sure why I came back. Once again, as it had in the past. the brass plaque caught my eye. I had noticed it during my conversation with Mary Ferrar but then overlooked it when Anne Boleyn had appeared and told me that her daughter, Queen Elizabeth, had become so disenchanted with the squabbling between the different branches of the church, she just withdrew the royal patronage from all religious houses, including Little Gidding. After Anne's visit my attention had been drawn away from the church to concentrate on the religious and political upheaval that convulsed England and so tragically involved this small place.

I was therefore not prepared for the next entries:

1614 - King James I, Patron
1651 - Parliament, Patron

It was not only that the first date was inaccurate: King James had ascended the throne in 1603, not 1614. But even more startling was the omission of any mention of King Charles I. He had ascended the throne upon his father's death in 1625 and lived until 1649. By all odds he had been the monarch most intimately involved with the life and fate of Little Gidding. Strange, as earlier mentioned, a window, known as "the King's Window," would commemorate the sad occasion when he arrived at night as

a fugitive seeking succor, but the brass plaque which listed
the Patrons as far back as the 12th century would omit his
name.

Not so strange, though, was the omission of the other man whose soldiers savaged this community during the
Civil War: Oliver Cromwell. He had become the "un-
crowned King of the Realm," and bore the official title as
Lord Protector of England, Scotland and Ireland. But during his reign he had so much difficulty with a fractious Parliament, in all probability he had no time for the religious
houses of England. Indeed, shortly after King Charles went
to his death with what some termed, "royal calm and Christian resignation," the Parliament established committees to
encourage the propagation of the faith (a term borrowed
from the Roman Catholic Church). Thus, the brass plaque
could well be accurate in listing Parliament as Patron of
this church beginning in the year those committees had
come into existence and had assumed the patronage of all
the religious houses in England.

Somehow, though, I was left with an empty feeling.
A sense that there was more to the story of this small place
than I had yet uncovered. I knew that those who had fled
Little Gidding had returned and continued to live here, else
how could I be sitting in this lovely sanctuary delving into
its past. Just then a voice spoke up:

"Behold an Israelite in whom there is no false-
hood."

It was a strong voice with a slight quaver in it. For a
moment I could not tell where it came from. Then I noticed
a figure sitting under the northwest Nave window. The window known as "The Nicholas Ferrar Window" beneath
which was the phrase from the gospel of St. John's which I
had just heard. I trembled with anticipation.

"No, I am not Nicholas Ferrar," answered the
voice. "I am Virginia Ferrar, the daughter of John Ferrar,

Nicholas' brother, and I come to tell you of the many things you have overlooked in your search for the truth about this place."

I was astonished. Very little has been written about John Ferrar; less about his children. The only things I unearthed were his involvement with the colony in Virginia and his efforts to help King Charles.

"I came to complete your story about Little Gidding. I can do so because I was born and lived my entire life at this place as did, John, junior, my older brother. My father named me after the colony in the New World which he had worked for early in his career and with which he never lost touch through all his years at Little Gidding. It is that part of the story of this community I will tell you first."

I liked the sound of Virginia's voice and the forthright manner of her speech. She captured my full attention.

"As you know, father was an officer in the London Company of Virginia which King James had chartered, and which later ran into financial difficulties that even Uncle Nicholas could not solve. When the entire family moved to Little Gidding, father continued his correspondence with the colonists in Virginia. As a child, he excited my imagination with stories of that far off place. As a teenager I began my own lively correspondence with several members of our family who had moved to Virginia during the troubled years in England. Later, I even began experimenting with growing silk-worms, using the mulberry bushes here at Little Gidding as a demonstration to the colonists that they could develop a silk-growing industry in Virginia instead of growing the 'noisome weed' tobacco. They didn't listen, of course, but I tried. In any case, I continued to correspond with them all of my life."

With that statement, the spirit of Virginia seemed to subside and just sat there looking at me. My own emotions were quite mixed. I was enthralled by her story but also filled with curiosity about other events that occurred at this strange and wonderful place. After awhile, I spoke up.

"Where did you go when you fled Little Gidding during the Civil War?" I asked her.

"As you know, father took over the leadership of Little Gidding after Uncle Nicholas died and did everything in his power to have the community carry on as before. Why, I even completed a copy of the Harmonies of the Bible when I was just twelve years old. My brother, Nicholas, was just as brilliant as Uncle Nicholas. He was the one who, just before he died at age twenty, translated the Harmonies of the Bible into several different languages for King Charles. He was so brilliant, so brilliant, it was such a waste when he died so young."

Virginia hesitated, deep in thought. I dared not pursue my question. But soon she spoke up:

"Uncle Nicholas had frequently spoken of the Dutch city of Leyden as a sanctuary for people of differing religious beliefs. As the war progressed, father became increasingly apprehensive for himself and the entire community so we packed up and fled to Holland afraid we might never see our home again."

Virginia's voice trailed off and I felt sorry for her. But I kept silent, not wishing to intrude on her private thoughts. After awhile she continued.

"As it came to pass, we stayed in Leyden less than three years. When we returned to Little Gidding there were just a few of us left. Some got married; others emigrated to

the colonies; others wanted safer abodes. Upon our return, Little Gidding consisted of our family: mother, father, John, junior, and me; also, father's sister, Susanna, and her husband, John Collett and their daughter, Mary. Very soon after we returned my mother, who never liked living in the country away from London, left and returned to that city. She never came back here; we had to visit her in London when we wanted to see her. Before father died, John, junior, married and his wife came to live with us. In time, only his family and I were the sole residents of the community. John, junior, became the last Lord of the Manor at Little Gidding."

"It was John, junior, who lived here the longest, and his son, Thomas, who became a clergyman and rector of Little Gidding, who restored the church very much as it is today."

I was almost lost in the sadness of hearing of the last of Little Gidding but I perked up at her last comment about the church. Excitedly, I asked her, *"Was the church different then than it is now?"*

"Yes", she answered seeming to come out of her own reverie. *"Over the years it fell into great disrepair. The round super-structure with the four windows in it, that appeared on the cover of that despicable pamphlet, 'The Arminian Nunnery,' was all but falling down."*

So the sketch on the pamphlet had been accurate. The church had had a round tower, as had the other Templar churches in England. I could not contain myself. *"Were there other features of the place that were accurately reported in that pamphlet?"* I asked her.

"No," she answered with asperity.

"Little Gidding was never an Arminian or any other kind of a nunnery. Several of Susanna's daughters and I chose not to get married but so did Queen Elizabeth. Uncle Nicholas chose a life of celibacy. But he was so ill all of his life, he always seemed to feel he was destined to die young."

"No," she continued, *"there was nothing ever done here other than an attempt to live a good Christian life. Uncle Nicholas felt to do that we had to pray often; go to church every day, and follow rigorous rules. But also that we had to serve others, as you have already mentioned."*

"But, I have to tell you we did not deserve to be called a "bridge to popery." We never acknowledged the Pope nor any of his henchmen in England. No, we were not in any sense an Arminian Nunnery."

At last, I thought, we have settled that issue. But I was still curious about the church so I decided to remind Virginia that she had started to tell me about her father and his son restoring the church, but she anticipated me.

"My nephew, Thomas Ferrar," Virginia went on, *"advised his father that the tower should be torn down and the width of the church reduced to just one aisle and its length shortened. To do this, the pulpit had to be removed and the west front moved. And, oh yes, I almost forgot. . . ."*

I trembled with anticipation.

". . . they dredged the pond and discovered the baptismal font and the cover with the fleur de lis and eight-pointed crosses, and the lectern with the claws damaged at the bottom. Everyone thought the soldiers had made off with them but they had laid, unnoticed, at the bottom of the pond for sixty-eight years!"

My heart leaped with joy. Finally, finally, some of the mystery of this place was being cleared up.

Virginia continued, *"So, except for the four windows which were installed later, the church that you now sit in was completed by my brother, John and his son, Thomas, in 1714, when John was 82 years old!"*

I looked around the church. I could not believe that I had found what I had long sought, the lifting of the last veil of mystery surrounding Little Gidding. I remembered the wording of the book on church architecture in the British Museum, *". . . the interior of the church at Little Gidding is strange and confusing118.3 . . . as is the foundation which is lost in antiquity. . . ."*

In my enthusiasm I almost ignored my visitor, the spirit of Virginia, who had done so much to clear up the mystery of this place. She was not to be ignored and spoke up very firmly.

"You have long heard that it is the woman who has the last word. I intend to continue that tradition. Except for Mary Ferrar, you have said almost nothing about the women of Little Gidding. I wish to remedy that oversight. After Mary died, her daughter, Susanna, took on the care of the house and the tiny community of saints. When she died and my Mother went back to London, it fell to me, a single woman, to continue to provide a woman's touch and love to the home. You see, dear sir, Nicholas Ferrar was every inch a sainted person but a home needs more than a saint, it needs the care of a woman. A hearth you must know is not a home but for the love of a woman. And so, Little Gidding was a place where hearth and heaven came together; a place that will never die. I tell you this from Paradise."

With those words the spirit of Virginia Ferrar departed. I took one last look around the lovely diminutive sanctuary, said a silent goodbye to all the wonderful spirits who had made my visits so memorable, and left.

*   *   *   *   *

The curious among you will want to know if the church at Little Gidding still survives. Not only is it surviving, it is thriving and it is as reverently beautiful today as it was when John Ferrar and his son, Thomas, refurbished it over two centuries ago. Indeed, the brass plaque reads:

Queen Elizabeth II, Patron

As one sits quietly in the small sanctuary, one of Eliot's poignant phrases takes on greater significance; this really is a place "where prayer has been made valid."

Outside the church, the community at Little Gidding is active and involved in a manner reminiscent of the days of Nicholas Ferrar: widows live there; several families work on the property; others work in the neighboring towns. As a group they seek to foster the feeling of the earlier Christian commune.

The story of Little Gidding will never end.—It will be with us until the end of time. Why? Because it is a living reminder of the durability of the Christian faith; a testament to the truth that behind the evil of the world is God in whom we can trust, and from whom we can summon the power to heal ourselves and others. The little church that refuses to die gives us what we need most: Hope.

REFERENCE NOTES

The material for this story can be found in the standard reference works about Little Gidding and the period in the history of England when the events described took place. There are several exceptions. To the best of my knowledge Catherine, Mary, Elizabeth I, or Anne Boleyn never visited Little Gidding. But who can deny their spirits may have? It is a reasonable speculation, too, that the Grand Masters of the Knights Templars and the Grand Priors of the Knight Hospitalers of the Order of St. John would visit their Preceptories in the hinterlands from time to time.

Furthermore, in researching the history of both the church and the community at Little Gidding, I found so many differing versions of actual events that it became difficult to determine just which version was the most accurate. This was true even in those instances where the writer claimed to be using authentic manuscripts found at Magdalene College, Cambridge University. Further, there is clear evidence that the original manuscript written by John Ferrar about the life of his brother, Nicholas, was lent to a friend and never seen again.

Thus, past histories of Little Gidding, like most other histories, is mostly seen through the eyes of the beholders.

In this story, however, Little Gidding is mostly seen through the spirits of the past. Who is to say that they do not know as much about this place as any person living today?

BIBLIOGRAPHY

BOOKS

Baigent, Michael, Richard Leigh and Henry Lincoln. *Holy Blood, Holy Grail* (London: Transworld Publishers, Ltd., 1982).

Barthel, Manfred, *The Jesuits* (New York: William Morrow & Co, 1982).

Bigland, Eileen, *Queen Elizabeth* (New York: Criterion Books, 1965).

Brown, John, *The English Puritans* (Cambridge: Cambridge University Press, 1912).

Charles, Elizabeth Drew, *T. S. Eliot: The Design of His Poetry* (New York: Scribner, 1949).

Durant, Will, *The Story of Civilization, Part VI, The Age of Reason Begins* (New York: Simon and Schuster, Inc., 1961).

Eliot, Esme Valarie, *Four Quartets* (Florida: Harcourt Brace Jovanovich, 1943/1971).

Ericson, Carolly, *Bloody Mary* (New York: Doubleday & Co., 1978).

Fraser, Antonia, *Cromwell* (Lomdon: Weidenfeld & Nicholson, 1973).

Gies, Frances, *The Knights in History* (New York: Harper & Row, 1884).

Howarth, David, *The Voyage of the Armada* (New York: Viking Press, 1981).

Lofts, Norah, *Anne Boleyn* (London: George Rainbird Ltd. 1979).

Maycock, Alan L., *Chronicles of Little Gidding* (London: S. P. C. K., 1954).
_____, *Nicholas Ferrar of Little Gidding* (London: Mowbray & Co., 1938).
Moncrief, M. C. Scott, *Kings and Queens of England* (New York: MacMillan Co., 1966).

Neale, J. E., *Queen Elizabeth I.* (London: Jonathan Cape, 1934).

Parker, Thomas W., *The Knights Templar in England* (Lubbock: Texas Tech. University, 1963).
Plowden, Alison, *Elizabeth Regina: The Age of Triumph* (New York: Times Books, 1980).

Ridley, Jasper, *Elizabeth: The Shrewdness of Virtue* (New York: Viking Press, 1987).
Routledge, Michael Reed and Kegan Paul, *The Age of Exuberance* (London: Routledge & Kegan Paul, 1986).
Rowley, Trevor, *The High Middle Ages* (London: Routledge & Kegan Paul, 1986).

Skipton, H. P. K., *Nicholas Ferrar* (London: A. R. Mowbray & Co. , 1907.
Smith, Grover Cleveland, *T. S. Eliot's Poetry and Plays* (Chicago: University of Chicago Press, 1956).
Strachey, Lytton, *Elizabeth and Essex* (New York: Harcourt Brace and World, 1979).

Traafe, John, *The Military and Religious Orders of the Middle Ages* (London: F. C. Woodhouse & Co., 1879).

Tuchman, Barbara, *A Distant Mirror* (New York: Alfred A. Knopf, 1978).

Wedgewood, C. V., *Oliver Cromwell* (London: Gerald Duckworth & Co., 1973).

White, Barbara, *Mary Tudor* (New York: MacMillan Co., 1935.

PAMPHLETS

Pamphlet 1 of St. John Historical Society, Lecture by Lionel Butler (London, 1981).

A History of the Parish of Great Gidding, Steeple Gidding and Little Gidding (Michael Wickes, 1979).

Little Gidding: An Illustrated Guide to the Church, Friends of Little Gidding and the Little Gidding Community.

The Story of Little Gidding, by A. L. Maycock (Little Gidding Community Press, 1980).

Little Gidding: Story and Guide by Robert Van de Weyer (London: Lamb Press, 1989).

The Arminian Nunnery and other 17th century accounts of Little Gidding (Little Gidding Community Press, 1987).

A Descriptive Guide to the Temple Church in London.

Britain's Kings and Queens (63 Reigns in 1100 Years) (London: Pitkin Books,. 1966).